1975

his book may be kept

W. H. AUDEN
as a Social Poet

W. H. AUDEN
as a Social Poet

FREDERICK BUELL

Cornell University Press

ITHACA AND LONDON

First published 1973 by Cornell University Press.
Published in the United Kingdom by Cornell University Press Ltd., 2–4 Brook Street, London W1Y 1AA.

International Standard Book Number 0-8014-0762-1
Library of Congress Catalog Card Number 72-12283

Printed in the United States of America by York Composition Co.

Librarians: Library of Congress cataloging information appears on the last page of the book.

For my parents

Acknowledgments

I am specially indebted to a number of Auden's critics: to Monroe Spears, for his comprehensive study of Auden's work; to John Bayley, for his sensitive description of Auden's style; and to Justin Replogle, for his work on the background of Auden's early poetry. I am more personally indebted to Arthur Mizener and Douglas Archibald of Cornell University for their consistently wise advice and encouragement throughout the preparation of this book.

I would also like to thank Random House, Inc., and Faber and Faber, Ltd., for permission to reprint excerpts from Auden's poetry and prose, and I am grateful to Methuen & Co., Ltd., and Curtis Brown, Ltd., for permission to reprint material from Christopher Isherwood's *Lions and Shadows*. Publishing information is given in the footnotes.

FREDERICK BUELL

Palo Alto, California

Contents

W. H. AUDEN
as a Social Poet

Introduction

It is the social aspect of W. H. Auden's verse that will ensure him an enduring and central place among major twentieth-century poets. No one, including William Butler Yeats, has managed to create verse responsive to the intellectual and emotional concerns of so large a cross section of reasonably intelligent twentieth-century social man; the modern realities against which Yeats often violently and yet inspiringly reacted are, in Auden's best work, the source of a poetry of moral balance and social integration, one in which an acutely ironic consciousness does not negate appreciation or enjoyment of the limited human goods still available to us in a time of historical crisis.

This book focuses on the years in which Auden's social vision was in its formative stage, the 1930's—the years of his flirtation with and abandonment of left-wing politics. This stage of the poet's work has received much critical comment; at worst, readers have either attempted to label Auden as a Marxist who, after his "apostasy," ceased to write good, "authentic" poetry, or tried to dismiss all his radical political verse as unimportant and only tangential to his literary development (a view that Auden himself has encouraged). Neither of these extremes helps to under-

1

stand Auden's development; his verse, if anything, improves after his "apostasy," and yet the improvement is one that only the social preoccupations of the thirties could have prepared him for.

The problem in discussing poetry and politics is, of course, how to go about it; for a critic concerned with writing as purely descriptive an analysis as possible, the relationships between a poem and its political circumstances and between a "revolutionary" poet and his society are exceedingly difficult to define. Clearly, one cannot rest content with determining what poems "say" about politics and then take that as an indication of what the poet "believes" at any point in time; to do so is to have a reductive understanding of the nature of both poetry and belief. Instead, one must pose a variety of complicated and indirect questions about the poem, the poet, and the political situation, questions that lead, by different ways, to a fuller understanding of how they are interrelated.

Such questions can be divided roughly into those concerned principally with literary matters and those concerned with political and historical circumstances. Of the first, the most trivial concern is the attempt to determine the arguments of specific poems; two political poets could, conceivably, embody the same ideological point in poems so different in style and spirit that one could not say they meant the same thing. One must also attempt to establish the information that an author's personal manner—that which makes any particular poem seem indubitably *his*—can yield about his personal political predispositions; further, one must consider how this manner relates to existing literary tradition in order to determine whether a poem is acting disruptively or revolutionarily in other ways than in its most overt content or intent. Of the second sort of question, the most simplistic is to ask how an individual work relates to its specific historical or political circumstances, an investigation of the poem in terms of its occasion. In addition, one must consider the possibilities open to a writer for relating imaginatively to the sources of political power; one must ask what political mythologies and social roles are available to individual writers in a particular society at a particular time.[1]

These two sets of questions are the basis for the first three chapters of this book. Auden began his career in an atmosphere of political and literary ferment: the poetic experimentalism and cultural-political speculation of Ezra Pound and T. S. Eliot were fashionable; the influence of continental avant-garde movements on English culture was just beginning; English writers and intellectuals were starting to take an active interest in English and European politics; the English government was being shaken by strikes, unemployment, and economic crisis; fascist movements were growing powerful in Europe; and the Marxist prophecy of a world revolution seemed to many to be on the brink of fulfillment. Auden was thus faced with developing a personal literary style and a coherent identity as an English writer in a time of historical crisis; as a writer peculiarly responsive to the spirit of his times and as one desirous of becoming a specifically "modern" poet, he was fully conscious of these two tasks.

The development of Auden's personal manner is exceed-

[1] See Thomas R. Edwards, *Imagination and Power* (New York: Oxford University Press, 1971), pp. 1–7, for a suggestive discussion of how an individual's relationship to politics may be understood as an imaginative act.

ingly difficult to trace; the range of his experimentation is so immense that one is almost reduced to saying that the only constants in his work are change and virtuosity. Auden often seems capable of "handling" any verse form and subject matter; as Christopher Isherwood, only somewhat unduly facetiously, wrote, "Auden is, and always has been, a most prolific writer. Problems of form and technique seem to bother him very little. You could say to him: 'Please write me a double ballade on the virtues of a certain brand of toothpaste, which also contains at least ten anagrams on the names of well-known politicians, and of which the refrain is as follows. . . .' Within twenty-four hours, your ballade would be ready—and it would be good."[2]

At the same time, Auden's work is marked by a well-defined, unmistakable signature. The word "Audenesque" is meaningful in characterizing a certain brash flamboyance and intellectual and formal virtuosity that runs throughout Auden's writing from his earliest, most privately eccentric work to his later attempts at explicitly public verse. Moreover, in political terms, the literary manner so described is of a definite order and tendency; it simultaneously subverts and supports English social and literary tradition. Its brashness is a form of parodic rebellion, whose very exhibitionism asks for social approval, something feasible in a tradition in which eccentricity, extravagance, and wit are recognized values. Its virtuosity in the use of ideas and literary forms serves playfully to subvert the seriousness of the

[2] Christopher Isherwood, "Some Notes on Auden's Early Poetry," *Auden* ed. Monroe Spears (Englewood Cliffs, N.J.: Prentice-Hall, 1964), pp. 11–12.

ideas and the authority of the forms, yet remains committed to rational analysis and literary structure, eschewing both romantic emotionalism and free-verse experimentalism. The development throughout the thirties of Auden's personal manner is marked by strong underlying continuity. Though argument and poetic form may vary greatly from poem to poem, and though Auden is working toward an ever more publicly accessible and traditionally sanctioned poetic style, his work maintains an internal tension between rebellious parodic gesture and tacit or overt appeal for general readership approval and participation.

Auden's search for a coherent identity as an explicitly modern English writer is a more complex phenomenon; it involves not only the content and manner of his work, but also the ways he found to relate to his society and immediate surroundings. As can be seen from all that has been written by his friends about his life in the early thirties, Auden created for himself a distinctive and appealing public personality; like his poetry, this public personality continued to develop throughout the decade. At Oxford, in Berlin, and later at Gresham School, he belonged to a loosely knit, but highly self-involved group, whose other important members were Christopher Isherwood, Edward Upward, Stephen Spender, and C. Day Lewis. The group created and elaborated a set of private fantasies, a self-enclosed schoolboy world they called "Mortmere." As the recent Auden critic Justin Replogle has shown, much of the obscurity of Auden's early work can be explained by the way it drew upon this private world; in terms of his political poetry, Mortmere is important in that Auden, at the beginning of his career, found a private group an imaginative necessity, not only because he is the kind of poet who needs first to have conceived of an audience for a poem, in order then to write, as he does, with one eye upon that audience, but also because, as a developing social poet, he was in need of a miniature society to act as a mediator between him and twentieth-century England.

With the publication of *Look, Stranger!* both the obscurity and the ambiguity of political reference of the early work had largely disappeared; much of the verse still came from private sources, but it had been made more publicly accessible and authoritative. One reason for this was Auden's growing commitment to writing coherent, polemical social verse based on a synthesis of the ideas of Marx and Freud; more important, however, was the fact that the early private group had aligned itself with forces at work in the larger social structure. The schoolboy rebelliousness of the Mortmere world became significantly interconnected with the new left-wing movement. One aspect of this movement was the development of a pseudo-revolutionary group of young intellectuals, for whom high-spirited, extravagant cultural activity could parallel and supplement Marxist revolutionary agitation. As the thirties progressed, these two forces seemed to work side by side ever more effectively; a self-conscious literary-political group of considerable importance developed, the size and influence of which could be measured by the success of an institution like the Left-Wing Book Club. The political situation of England and the Continent actually fostered the growth of such a group; "enlightened" members of a crisis-ridden liberal society watched the development, in Europe, of what seemed the final confrontation between extreme right and extreme left, between Fascism and Communism, a confrontation objectified at the end of the thirties in the Spanish Civil War. Nor was it insignificant that Europe and not England provided the theater for the confrontation; there was, in England, the breathing space necessary for the development of a culture of dissent.

The war in Spain provided the last occasion for an uninhibited release of these radical cultural-political energies. The victory of the fascist-supported side and the gradual realization of some of the more grotesque methods the Communists used to gain power within the Republican faction considerably blunted the idealistic fervor of the left wing, and Englishmen of all political leanings had to begin to unite to face a second world war. Auden's last major left-wing political poem, "Spain, 1937," was written about the Spanish Civil War; the poem has an uneasiness that is due in large part to Auden's attempt to blend the youthful iconoclastic extravagance of his literary-political group with the unyielding facts of an imminently tragic political occasion.

Shortly after the Republican defeat in Spain, Auden committed what some critics have called his "apostasy": he abandoned his English literary-political group, gave up his advocacy of Marxist social theory, emigrated to America, and soon experienced a religious conversion, becoming absorbed in existentialist Christian theology. With this step, which represents Auden's last major change in "beliefs," he gained access to a far greater range of ideas and assurance of poetic voice than ever before. The change, however, was far less radical than many have understood it to be. His concern with writing social verse did not cease, nor did the basis for that verse change as much as the terms "radical" and "middle of the road" or "conservative" would imply; he went from writing as a spokesman for a growing radical group—one composed of many of the favored sons of the old order—to becoming a spokesman for a half-mythical group of right-minded, well-meaning, harried citizens of the modern bureaucratic, philistine age, a group irreverent toward and out of sympathy with the "managers" who control such a society. The parodic rebelliousness of the early poetry remains in a muted form: it comes from a self-consciously apolitical standpoint, not allied with any active ideology. The sense of writing as a spokesman for a specific group—a group with strong and highly fanciful Arcadian overtones—remains; the group, however, has expanded to include most disaffected twentieth-century men, and it is held together now only by its echoes of a social Arcadia, not by the hope of a social millennium. To see that the Auden of the early poems and the Auden of the later poems are not so different as it might seem, one need only place poems like "Out on the lawn I lie in bed" and "In Praise of Limestone" or "Brothers when the sirens roar" and "Under Which Lyre" side by side; though these poems are radically different in theme, their similarity of tone is remarkable. Auden's political alignment and argumentation of the thirties have been abandoned; much of the spirit that informed them, however, remains intact.

1. The Rational Fantasy

W. H. Auden's *Poems* (1930) and *The Orators* (1932) were books that seemed, at the time of their appearance, refreshingly and startlingly novel; though they had much in common with T. S. Eliot's *The Waste Land*, the first great English poetic document of a self-consciously modern age, they were the products of a poetic sensibility of a far different nature. *The Waste Land* and Auden's early work shared the assumption that English and European society was diseased and perhaps moribund; Auden's books, however, treated that theme in a surprisingly high-spirited and energetic manner, in a style unmarked by the brooding desolation of Eliot's poem. Similarly, though both poets' writings were intellectually and literarily sophisticated, making wide use of English and European cultural traditions, the ways in which they incorporated such material were scarcely comparable; the breadth of the literary and intellectual reference of *The Waste Land* was meant ultimately to show the decline of the cultural tradition of the Western world, while Auden's work aimed at a parodic re-evaluation and, to a certain extent, reanimation of old traditions. Finally, although both men were involved in daringly experimental writing, Auden delighted in displaying his inventiveness, whereas Eliot showed no such infatuation with either surprise or novelty.

One of the most vivid and revealing examples of all these traits—Auden's high spirits, his concern for themes of political and social relevance, his parodic use of literary tradition, and his experimentalism—is "Journal of an Airman," the most intriguing section of *The Orators*. A close examination of that piece will reveal the sensibility that lies behind all of Auden's early work. Although it is one of the more lucid sections of *The Orators*, the "Journal" is characteristically difficult to interpret in any definitive way. It is a bizarre mixture of structure and confusion, of the fantastic and the comprehensible; a private journal of a mythological "Airman," put together from diverse literary, non-literary, public, and private sources, it functions like a riddle, waking in readers both a strong desire to solve it and an amused frustration at the impossibility of ever completely doing so. The structure of the "Journal" appears at first to be tantalizingly simple: it records the struggle between the Airman and his deadly enemy, a struggle that progresses from the secret violence and elaborate strategies of guerilla warfare to the brink of a surrealistic, nearly apocalyptic confrontation. One thinks that, if he could just pin down who or what the Airman and his enemy are and just what their conflict stands for, he would have the "answer" to the puzzle.

The appeal of the work to its contemporary readers was of a peculiarly political nature; not only did it seem to be treating political themes, but it also appeared to be itself a blow against the existing literary and political establishments. As a result, a great effort was made to allegorize the

"Journal" in terms of recognizable types, and, in the course of such speculation, the Airman was glossed as a fascist, a Marxist revolutionary, and a romantic rebel of both the left and the right. The very number and contradictory nature of these solutions suggest that no such single explanation is really adequate, and a short look at the "Journal" will show this to be indeed the case. There is not enough unambiguous detail about the social status of the Airman or his enemy to justify calling the former either a facist or Marxist rebel. Although in a general sense the enemy does seem to represent the upper classes, this category remains far too vague to attempt to align him with any political ideology; correspondingly, the nature of the Airman's own political organization is left entirely unspecified.

To call the Airman a romantic rebel and not to try to determine whether he is of the right or left is more acceptable, because his conflict with the "enemy" then does not need to be particularized in explicitly political terms. Such a character would be roughly similar to the Airman, that is, a rebel of whom the most striking and interesting aspect is his sensibility, who is essentially impractical, often deludes himself, and is greatly concerned with symbolic gesture. A specific description of the Airman's "rebellion," however, is almost impossible: the details of the "Journal" are too complicated. Since the whole atmosphere of the piece is paranoid, it is never certain whether a detail is indicative of the Airman's own neurosis or of the enemy's sinister nature, whether the detail describes an internal or external "reality." Examples of this ambiguity are provided by the section "Of the Enemy," in which the enemy is characterized by a long list of attributes, more or less meaningful. Some of his defining traits seem to indicate that he is a particular social type, a member of a neurotic but objective society: "Three enemy catchwords—insure now—keep smiling—safety first."[1] Other traits, however, appear more darkly significant: "Three signs of an enemy letter—underlining—parentheses in brackets—careful obliteration of cancelled expressions."[2] The enemy is portrayed (by implication) as sick: he underlines to make what might be false emphasis, is intricate and devious of mind, and rigorously censors his own words. But the sinister aura surrounding these characteristics and the sense that they are threatening to the Airman, combined with the Airman's choice of such devious and neurotic traits as distinguishing marks for an enemy, suggest that the sickness is perhaps the Airman's own.

If we then abandon the attempt to allegorize the Airman in terms of political-social reality, the results are far more encouraging. In recent years, a number of revealing outside sources have been brought to bear upon the "Journal"; the most important discovery was of a passage in Christopher Isherwood's *Lions and Shadows*, in which Isherwood distinguishes between the Truly Strong Man and the Truly Weak Man:

"The truly strong man," calm, balanced, aware of his

[1] "Journal of an Airman," *The Orators: An English Study* (New York: Random House, 1967), p. 42. Selections from *The Orators* are reprinted by permission of Faber and Faber, Ltd., and Random House, Inc., © copyright, 1966, by W. H. Auden, copyright 1934, by The Modern Library Inc., copyright renewed, 1961, by W. H. Auden.

[2] Ibid.

strength, sits drinking quietly in the bar; it is not necessary for him to try and prove to himself that he is
not afraid, by joining the Foreign Legion, seeking out
the most dangerous wild animals in the remotest tropi-
cal jungles, leaving his comfortable home in a snow-
storm to climb the impossible glacier. In other words,
the Test exists only for the Truly Weak Man: no matter whether he passes it or whether he fails, he cannot
alter his essential nature. The Truly Strong Man trav-
els straight across the broad America of normal life,
taking always the direct, reasonable route. But "America" is just what the truly weak man, the neurotic hero,
dreads. And so with immense daring, with an infinitely
greater expenditure of nervous energy, money, time,
physical and mental resources, he prefers to attempt
the huge northern circuit, the laborious, terrible north-
west passage, avoiding life; and his end, if he does not
turn back, is to be lost forever in the blizzard and the
ice.[3]

The concept of the Airman as the neurotic hero engaged
in great struggle, the purpose of which is to avoid normal
life, explains the basic structure of the "Journal"; the enemy would be the product of the Airman's own imagination, a delusion self-created out of an indifferent normality,
and the final conflict would be by definition surreal, the
deadly struggle of a disordered mind with its own halluci-
natory imagination. Thus, throughout the course of events

[3] Norfolk: New Directions, 1947, pp. 207–208. The passage was
first applied to Auden by W. Sellers in "New Light on Auden's
The Orators," PMLA, 82 (1967), 460–461.

recorded in the "Journal," we are observing the progressive deterioration of a neurotic sensibility; as the Airman himself recognizes at the end, his "whole life has been mistaken, progressively more and more complicated, instead of finally simple."[4] It seems, at the end of the "Journal," that the Airman has come to a self-awareness which will free him temporarily from his spiral into insanity:

> My incredible blindness, with all the facts staring me in the face, not to have realised these elementary truths.
>
> 1. The power of the enemy is a function of our resistance, therefore
> 2. The only efficient way to destroy it—self-destruction, the sacrifice of all resistance, reducing him to the state of a man trying to walk on a frictionless surface.
> 3. Conquest can only proceed by absorption of, *i.e.* infection by, the conquered. The true significance of my hands. 'Do not imagine that you, no more than any other conqueror, escape the mark of grossness.' They stole to force a hearing.[5]

The Airman's reference to his hands, and by implication to several of his neurotic symptoms such as kleptomania and masturbation-anxiety, seems to indicate that he has finally

---

[4] "Journal," p. 58. The idea stems from D. H. Lawrence's *Fantasia of the Unconscious*, a chief source for the "Journal": "the more problems you solve, the more will spring up, their fingers at their nose, making a fool of you." D. H. Lawrence, *Psychoanalysis and the Unconscious and Fantasia of the Unconscious* (New York: Viking, 1960), p. 182.

[5] "Journal," p. 58.

conquered his disorder; the last entry in the "journal" bears out this interpretation:

> 3:40 a.m.
>> Pulses and reflexes, normal.
>> Barometric reading, 30.6.
>> Mean temperature, 34° F.,
>> Fair. Some cumulus cloud at 10,000 feet. Wind easterly and moderate.
>> Hands in perfect order.[6]

That the Airman's attempt to conquer himself by yielding to and absorbing that self as something positive is further indicated by an essay written by Auden about a more famous Airman, T. E. Lawrence:

> We can't go back on it [self-consciousness]. But its demands on our little person and its appetites are so great that most of us, terrified, try to escape or make terms with it, which is fatal. As a pursuer it is deadly. Only by the continuous annihilation of the self by the Identity, to use Blake's terminology, will it bring us the freedom we wish for, or, in T. E. Lawrence's own phrase, 'Happiness comes in absorption'.[7]

The conclusion of the "Journal" is equally well described by D. H. Lawrence:

> When I say to myself, "I am wrong," knowing with sudden insight that I am wrong, then this is the whole self speaking, the Holy Ghost. . . . When at last, in

[6] Ibid., p. 60.

[7] As quoted in Herbert Greenberg, *Quest for the Necessary* (Cambridge: Harvard University Press, 1968), p. 56.

all my storms, my whole self speaks, then there is a
pause. The soul collects itself into pure silence and isolation—perhaps after much pain. The mind suspends its
knowledge, and waits. The psyche becomes strangely
still. And then, after a fresh pause, there is fresh beginning, fresh life adjustment.[8]

At the end of the "Journal," then, the Airman conquers his
neurosis temporarily, and for that time he becomes the
Truly Weak Man turned heroic; as such, he is still not the
Truly Strong Man, a type far from attractive in the way
he is able to go "straight across the broad America of normal life, taking always the direct, reasonable route." Instead, the Airman faces the Test and, at least temporarily,
transcends the dialectic.

This sketchy review of criticism has done no more than
to set the "Journal" in the roughest kind of order; many
of the individual entries remain as undecipherable as ever.[9]
For the present purposes, such a sketch is adequate; it establishes quite clearly the nature of the dialectic in both
the "Journal" and in Auden's early poetry. As Isherwood's
description of the Truly Weak Man and Truly Strong
Man reveals, Auden is playing between two fairly clear
poles, between an interpretation of fantasy as neurotic, self-
defeating, yet creative, and a concept of reality which, although stable, reasonable, and perhaps even enlightened, is
alas profoundly dull. Thus, the Airman, in the earlier por-
tions of the "Journal," engages in a neurotic polemic against

[8] *Fantasia of the Unconscious*, p. 165.

[9] For the best reading of the "Journal," one to which I am much
indebted, see John Fuller, *A Reader's Guide to W. H. Auden*
(New York: Farrar, Strauss, and Giroux, 1970), pp. 62–69.

a reason that, to him, represents limitation of vision, emotional paralysis, and a stifling of creativity; the cramped and obsessively logical nature of his polemic ironically reveals that he, far more than his enemy, is the one suffering from the agony of rationality. At the end of the "Journal," then, he temporarily transcends the Weak-Strong dialectic and conquers his suffering; but this victory reduces his consciousness to the level of pure fact, to a state of mind that is, on the surface, unfortunately close to unimaginative normality (the "broad America") and that expresses itself in the merely factual diary entries of his last days or, better, in silence. Auden's comment in the essay on T. E. Lawrence does suggest that this transcendence is something far better than normality, for it involves the *continuous* annihilation of the self by the Identity; with the Airman, though, we have no evidence that such violence in stability is achieved with any permanency, for we leave him just on the morning of his Final Conflict.

The dialectic between a diseased fantasy and a stable but dull reality can be seen, in essence, as a simplified interpretation of Freud; it is based on the devastating reevaluation of both imagination and normality that is contained in the remarkably gloomy little axiom, "A happy person never phantasies, only an unsatisfied one."[10] At the same time, this dialectic has had an almost unbelievable political effect in the twentieth century, and this fact has led many readers to discover in the "Journal" an explicitly political allegory.

---

[10] Sigmund Freud, "The Writer and Day-Dreaming," *The Standard Edition of the Complete Psychological Works of Sigmund Freud,* ed. James Strachey (London: The Hogarth Press, 1959), IX, 146.

It is thus important to consider briefly at the outset just what this dialectic, in political terms, consists of; in doing so, questions will be raised that will be dealt with throughout this book, questions implicit in the often self-contradictory phenomenon of a cultural revolution.

The belief most basic to this dialectic is simple: the artistic imagination has come to be seen as something profoundly subversive, subversive of both the normality of the individual and that of society, and, more generally, subversive of the Real. Of course, as soon as one adopts this view and tries to *use* it, one is no longer dealing with the imagination; instead, one has entered the realm of tendentious fantasy, which, for all its rebellion, is well aware of the claims of its far more powerful but far less charming enemy, the Real.

We commonly encounter two quite different but related forms of imaginative revolt. The rebellion of Imagination can be a shattering, transforming, and intensely vital experience, in which both the self and the world are undone and (hopefully) remade; it is a revolt in the name of some unnamed, dark, and vitalistic power, one simultaneously human and suprahuman (or subhuman, depending on how one regards that power), and it emphasizes the potentially violent nature of creativity. That Auden was, as a young poet, interested in this kind of experience is amply evidenced by his reading of D. H. Lawrence and his comments about T. E. Lawrence; at the same time, this interest remained only an interest, for Auden's main concern was not to achieve such experience for himself but to formulate it and use it as an idea. Thus, in his essay on T. E. Lawrence, Auden is quick to try to place "absorption" in the context of an intellectual tradition, linking it to William Blake, and, in the "Journal," the ideas of D. H. Lawrence are used as ideas, as material for a seemingly allegorical fantasy.

In contrast to the rebellion of Imagination, the rebellion of Fantasy is best described as rebellion of a willed, conscious excrescence of idea and expression, one intended to act upon the defenders of Reality in a manner titillating, provoking, annoying, or, in its extreme form, outright offensive; as such, it falls most naturally into a dialectic of youth against age. The young, the fertile and unformed, resist definition by their elders, those who have already decided upon themselves and reality and who are, as a result, internally dead; the dialectic is itself in large part a creation of the rebellious fantasy, for the types upon which it rests —creative youth and stagnant, oppressive maturity—are basically caricatures. Such rebelliousness of Fantasy has a relatively limited but highly interesting vocabulary. It is first and foremost exhibitionistic and irresponsible; and it encourages judgment of itself as such. It delights in its own eccentricity and disruptiveness; yet it reveals itself in all it does as unreal, consciously fantastic, and, as a result, tends most naturally toward expression through caricature. Most important, its clearest self-image is that of something that fights small rear-guard actions against boredom and meaning, quite conscious of the fact that these are only rear-guard actions; if it pools forces (as it commonly does) with something far more earnestly revolutionary than itself, for example, a Marxist ideology, it may avoid the gay nullity of mere nonsense, may subject its own anarchistic inventiveness to an external, rational control, and may thus become a small but heady weapon in a genuine struggle.

It should be clear that the rebelliousness of spirit one senses in the "Journal" is basically of disruptive fantasy. The mythology of the Truly Strong and Truly Weak Man is itself a creation of such fantasy; Isherwood indicates that the Truly Weak Man was invented originally in opposition to a notion of strength formulated by a homicidal paranoiac. The two categories were, moreover, elaborated in a series of group fantasies called the "Mortmere" fantasies, which were shared most closely by Isherwood, Auden, and another friend, Edward Upward, and which became for them not only a form of private communication, but also a framework within which they could order their early intellectual interests; the fantasies were so well developed that we can, with Justin Replogle, refer to them as the Auden "gang myth."[11] As we shall see in Chapter 2, it is this "gang myth" that provides an explanation of the peculiar tendentiousness of Auden's early work; here it is sufficient to observe that the "Journal" is not just a construction of fantasy, but also a use of fantasy to make a palpable hit against some imperfectly defined social target. Indeed, one of the chief tasks of the literary politics of the thirties was the definition of that target.

[11] "The Gang Myth in Auden's Early Poetry," *Journal of English and Germanic Philology*, 61 (1962), 481–495. Replogle also shows in some detail how many of the more obscure places in Auden's early work can be explicated with regard to the "gang myth" and how traces of this myth can be found not only in the work of Auden and Upward, but also in the work of several additional friends, C. Day Lewis and Rex Warner.

The self-conscious willfulness of Auden's fantasy reveals itself not only in the theme and tone of the "Journal"; the way in which it was conceived and written also indicates Auden's penchant for elaborate and playful artistic contrivance. If the effect of the "Journal" is very much like that of a riddle, from the standpoint of composition as well the "Journal" has much in common with the riddle form. Both are solved by a process of unraveling, by sorting out and identifying the pieces so that one sees at last the rationale behind their combination; similarly, their creation implies a conscious and clever "putting together" of the material. Since such planned construction is so unusual and seemingly unpoetic a form of creation—one has to fling oneself into the very teeth of Coleridge's "mechanical Fancy"—it will be important to an understanding and appraisal of Auden's art to try to define more clearly just what it involves.

Most important is the choice of a framework which will not just include an interesting variety of experience, but will also absorb it thoroughly into the realm of the tantalizingly fantastic. The figure of the Airman is a remarkable triumph in this respect; through such a neurotic, hallucinating, highly intellectual figure, Auden was able to unify a number of quite dissimilar elements. First, the Airman was a figure of the popular imagination; at the time Auden wrote the "Journal," flying was a matter of daily public sensation. Charles Lindbergh was still vivid in the memory of most people, young and old, and more recently, in 1930, Amy Johnson had made her sensational flight to Australia.[12]

[12] In this connection, the Airman's marvelously psychotic comment, "There is something peculiarly horrible about the idea of women pilots" (p. 50), takes on a topical meaning.

How the airplane might be used in modern warfare was a question that was just becoming important; the thought of massive destruction coming from the air was now a nightmarish possibility. A similar, but more private source for the Airman was T. E. Lawrence. More generally, the "Journal" was taken as a political allegory; still another level was the psychological, and it is possible that Auden, in the creation of a schoolboyish atmosphere for the "Journal," had in mind the comment by Freud, "Thus aviation, too, which in our day is at last achieving its aim, has its infantile erotic roots."[13] Most important, though, was the way Auden, in putting the Airman in the midst of a conflict in which intellectual subtlety was one of the chief weapons, was able to include a wide range of incidental material, from Mendelian charts to Icelandic runes to diagrams from perceptual psychology; because of the nature of the context he had created for this material, he was able to give it a peculiarly sinister urgency.[14]

The best indication of how this variety of material was brought together and why such construction was appealing to Auden is given us in a comment by Isherwood about the genesis of *Paid on Both Sides:*

> On his [Auden's] recommendation, I now began, for the first time, to read *Grettir* and *Burnt Njal,* which

[13] "Leonardo DaVinci and a Memory of his Childhood," *Complete Psychological Works*, XI, 126.

[14] There are also a number of more incidental identifications for the Airman; as Joseph Warren Beach has pointed out, *Luftmensch* (literally, "Airman") in Yiddish means roughly "Johnny Head-in-Air," and Auden himself commented that "The closest modern equivalent to the Homeric hero is the ace fighter pilot" (cited by Fuller, p. 62).

he had with him in his suitcase. These warriors, with their feuds, their practical jokes, their dark threats conveyed in puns and riddles and deliberate understatements ("I think this day will end unluckily for some, but chiefly for those who least expect harm"): they seemed so familiar—where had I met them before? Yes, I recognized them now: they were the boys at our preparatory school. Weston [Auden] was pleased with the idea: we discussed it a good deal, wondering which of our schoolfellows best corresponded to the saga characters. In time, the school-saga world became for us a kind of Mortmere—a Mortmere founded upon our preparatory-school lives, just as the original Mortmere had been founded upon my life with Chalmers [Edward Upward] at Cambridge. About a year later, I actually tried the experiment of writing a school story in what was a kind of hybrid language composed of saga phraseology and schoolboy slang. And soon after this, Weston produced a short verse play in which the two worlds are so confused that it is almost impossible to say whether the characters are epic heroes or members of a school O. T. C.[15]

Isherwood suggests a rather novel approach to literary genre that is characteristic of much of Auden's early work, most clearly *Paid on Both Sides*, *The Orators*, and *The Dance of Death*. What Isherwood suggested to Auden was a juxtaposition, outrageous in terms of traditional notions of genre, of two predefined and radically unlike sources, two "worlds" separated by centuries and, on the surface at

[15] Isherwood, pp. 192–193.

least, vastly disparate in mood and content. Yet just this disparity is the fruitful element; it makes the combination pleasing, rich in possibilities for parody, and suggestive of further development. The emphasis is heavily on form: the two "worlds" are best seen as literary genres, and mixing them is like mixing, for example, the pastoral and the naturalistic modes, in that a large number of the possible effects are suggested by the simple juxtaposition of their traditional elements.

In the "Journal of an Airman," one encounters a wealth of experimentation with the heuristic use of genre, the "juxtaposition of disparate coordinates"—to adapt one of Randall Jarrell's categories for Auden's rhetoric to the consideration of structure.[16] One such mixture of genre is the fusion of the Icelandic and the schoolboy worlds; a further play with disparate sources is indicated by Auden in his introduction to the 1967 edition of *The Orators:*

> The stimulus to writing *Journal of an Airman* came from two sources, Baudelaire's *Intimate Journals,* which had just been translated by Christopher Isherwood, and a very dotty semi-autobiographical book by General Ludendorff, the title of which I have forgotten. And over the whole work looms the shadow of that dangerous figure, D. H. Lawrence the Ideologue, author of *Fantasia of the Unconscious* and those sinister novels *Kangaroo* and *The Plumed Serpent.*[17]

That the list of sources is exceptionally just can be seen

[16] "Changes in Attitude and Rhetoric in Auden's Poetry," *The Southern Review,* 7 (1941), 340.
[17] Page vii.

from an analysis of a short passage. The second entry in the Airman's diary is typical of his schematic mind:

> The effect of the enemy is to introduce inert velocities into the system (called by him laws or habits) interfering with organisation. These can only be removed by friction (war). Hence the enemy's interest in peace societies.[18]

The combination of a rather unusual use of logical propositions with the diary form is to be found in the *Intimate Journals;* General Ludendorff would have been one stimulus to the creation of the myth of battle;[19] and Lawrence's notion of the vital organization of the personality, as expounded in *Psychoanalysis and the Unconscious* and *Fantasia of the Unconscious,* provides the general idea of the diary entry.

As with *Paid on Both Sides,* what first comes to mind is the disparate nature of the given sources: Lawrence and Baudelaire, both highly respectable literary forebears, and, the joker in the pack, General Ludendorff. Ludendorff would have been attractive to Auden for a number of reasons; the most important of these is the fact that he combines in his person what the Airman also does, namely, insanity and an involvement in politics and society. After World War I, Ludendorff became progressively dottier;

[18] Ibid., p. 31.

[19] It is possible that Auden knew quite a bit more about Ludendorff than this one "dotty . . . book" (identified by Fuller as *The Coming War* [1931]), for Ludendorff was a well-known and controversial character when Auden was in Berlin in 1929. The notion of the sinister nature of peace societies was something Ludendorff expounded in a number of his works.

he allied himself for a while with Hitler and then turned against him, into what represented, if anything, a deeper insanity, though a more ineffectual one. He did predict that there would be soon a second major war on German soil; the analysis that lay behind his prediction, however, was more than a little mad. Ludendorff believed that German blood was being threatened by a conspiracy of the *Überstaatliche Mächte* of Jews, Freemasons, and Papists; in short, Ludendorff had come to a fascist belief combined with a thoroughgoing paranoia, an obsession with the shiftiest of possible enemies, an unreal enemy which was everywhere about, within both Germany and his own mind.

In more particular ways, Ludendorff's character appears in the "Journal"; he provided Auden with individual ideas, such as the threatening nature of peace societies, and with the general language of battle, that of enemies, shock troops, troop dispositions, and the technique of outlining day by day the increasing horrors of war. Similarly, one can view some of the Airman's bizarre logic (his use, for example, of diagrams to reveal the enemy's presence) as a variation on the mad symbolic and numerological proofs that Ludendorff frequently used to lay bare the machinations of the Jews and Freemasons. Finally, it should be pointed out that the general tenor of Ludendorff's character would have been interesting to Auden, for Ludendorff was, in many ways, a kind of caricature of himself; he once made an escape under cover of a false beard and blue spectacles and put on quite a comic show during the Munich Beer Hall *Putsch* of 1923.[20]

[20] See D. J. Goodspeed, *Ludendorff: Genius of World War II*

The Airman, however, is not another Ludendorff; he is a more complicated and weaker character, filled with self-doubts and fantasies. The influence of Charles Baudelaire's *Intimate Journals* is evident in Auden's use of the diary form to express the self-doubting, tortured, strangely analytic spirit of the Airman. In Baudelaire, there are abstract, almost desperately urged precepts that are quite similar to the Airman's commands to himself; for example, Baudelaire writes the short prescription "Of the vaporisation and centralization of the *Ego*. Everything depends on that."[21] Similarly, Baudelaire will put in almost syllogistic form matter that seems far removed from the province of logic, thus making logic sound like psychological compulsion. More important is the aura of the introverted and obscure mind; as T. S. Eliot remarks in the introduction to Isherwood's translation, "There are short phrases and single words which seem memoranda for thoughts, unknown to us, to be developed later" and the comment is equally applicable to Auden's "Journal."[22]

Auden's most striking use of the *Intimate Journals* is his literal adoption of the sudden reversal at the end; Baudelaire, in what is the most focused and absorbing section of his journal, urges himself to a dramatic change, to the abandonment of a life of sloth and idle dreaming: "How many have been the presentiments and signs sent me already by God that it is high time to act, to consider the present

---

(Boston: Houghton Mifflin, 1966), for an amusing account of the incident.

[21] Trans. C. Isherwood (London: Blackmore Press, 1930), p. 99.

[22] Ibid., p. 25.

moment as the most important of all moments and to take for my *everlasting delight* my accustomed torment, that is to say, to work!"[23] Then, under the section "*Hygiene. Conduct. Morality*." he gives himself such desperate directives as "Jeanne 300, my mother 200, myself 300–800 francs a month. To work from six o'clock in the morning, fasting, until midday. To work blindly, without aim, like a madman. We shall see the result."[24] One is reminded of the Airman's turn, after his sudden reversal, to such precepts as "Read Mifflin on Air Currents" or, more significantly, "Destroy all letters, snapshots, lockets, etc., of E."[25] The last entries, in contrast to Baudelaire, portray a quieting of mind: the "Journal" ends as he takes off on the morning of the final battle with the comment that his hands are now in perfect order. Moreover, the Airman differs in a general way from his Baudelairean model, in that his struggle involves the fantasy-construction of the enemy and his neurosis is indicated by the rather abstractly and wittily conceived symptoms of stealing hands, horror of female pilots, and hatred of his immediate family; in Baudelaire's diary, the situation is not turned into such fantasy or clearly organized pathology, but rather represents the existential problem of a sloth which approaches acedia in the intensity with which it is felt. What has been adopted, then, is essentially a mode of diary writing and the technique of sudden reversal at the end, a reversal which gives immediate point to the rest of the diary.

Several points are now clear about the nature of these

[23] Ibid., pp. 99–100.
[24] Ibid., p. 103.
[25] "Journal," p. 59.

two influences on Auden. First, an important way in which the sources were interesting to him is essentially formal; it is characteristic, for example, that Auden would have responded so literally to the reversal at the end of the *Intimate Journals* as to have constructed his whole "Journal" around one—the Baudelaire model seems to serve the same function in the writing of the "Journal" as the prior choice of a certain kind of poetic form does to the creation of a poem, a function partly that of an artificial framework and partly that of a heuristic device. Second—and heuristic in a more general way—is the fact that the two influences represent, as did Isherwood's suggestion for *Paid on Both Sides*, contrary "worlds," taken from widely different areas of experience and suggestive through their juxtaposition of a great deal of the material in the "Journal." The framework thereby achieved allowed Auden to incorporate a wide variety of other sources in such a way as to draw them into a strange and interesting new context. The propositions

> There is a centre and a circumference, and between them is awareness of interdependence—sympathy.
> The enemy attempts to disturb this awareness by theories of partial priority.[26]

put a schematically indicated philosophical idea, done in the manner of Baudelaire, into a new, slightly paranoid context derivable from Ludendorff; the idea suddenly alters its nature and is given, despite its schematic character, a new concreteness (it is a target of the enemy's attack) and, instead of its philosophical neutrality, a new, urgent

[26] Ibid., p. 33.

point (the enemy's destruction of it means significant loss). All it has taken to alter our feelings toward the abstract proposition so radically is the reference to the enemy; that reference has put the proposition in the context of a world that does not even have to be clearly defined in order to have effect. All that is necessary is that "enemy" refer us to something we sense to be a composite of gestures, situations, and feelings that have a formal coherence so close that one term will call forth the general atmosphere of this "world." The kinds of worlds most susceptible to this method of evocation are sharply defined, clearly limited, and so much of a genre that they are perceived as fictional; thus Auden is attracted to the Icelandic sagas, to popular literature such as spy and detective stories, and to psychoanalytic case studies, which may be read as a distinctive literary genre; and he often brings these into conjunction with the schoolboy world, both because that world is itself distinct, limited, and perceived as fictional (the masters quickly become characters rather than people and, partly due to the ritualistic nature of the public school, small details quickly assume mythic significance and atmospheric quality) and because the schoolboy world is one in which this kind of manufacturing and use of fantasy is common.

The third source that Auden mentioned as underlying the "Journal," D. H. Lawrence, is not so interesting in a discussion of *how* the "Journal" was constructed; Lawrence provided the fantasy of the "Journal" with a rational structure, both directly, in that Auden made use of *Fantasia of the Unconscious* for certain ideas, and indirectly, in that Lawrence played a major part in the elaboration of the dialectic between the Truly Weak and the Truly Strong

Man. The fact that Auden drew on Lawrence is of great
interest in connection with the observation *that* the "Journal" was constructed; to use Lawrence as material for the
structure of a rational fantasy is quite alien to the spirit of
Lawrence, the writer who spent his life mocking minds
preoccupied with their ideas and limited by their rationality. From this standpoint, Auden's description of Lawrence
as a "dark shadow" hovering over *The Orators* is extreme;
the way Auden used Lawrence robs that "dark shadow" of
its vitalistic mystery. Instead, we may make an observation
that remains relevant to most of Auden's poetry throughout the thirties: his use of outside "truth" for the structure
of his poetry comes as much from the fact that this truth
provides his fantasy with the necessary limitation of a structure as it does from any genuineness of belief in the particular truth he is using at any one time. A comment by
Stephen Spender is instructive in this connection: "So with
the other answers: from psychology to Communism to
Christianity; they remain a little arbitrary and perhaps the
root of this arbitrariness is the poet's own isolation."[27] Although poetic isolation does not seem to be in any way a
crucial factor in Auden's life or work (the number of literary friendships he has maintained testify to the opposite),
Spender's choice of the word "answer" to characterize Auden's beliefs is extremely apt; it expresses just what many
readers have felt about Auden's work, namely that his
poems are, even when they seem to be making personal
statements, brilliant but contrived poetic arguments. The
nature of Auden's poetic beliefs is a large and difficult

[27] *World within World* (London: Hamish Hamilton, 1951),
p. 55,

topic, and a full discussion of it will be postponed until a later chapter; it is possible to make one further observation now. The fact that Auden's "answers" are held as "answers" and thus in a kind of pragmatic abstraction from personal sentiment is a principal condition for one of Auden's most attractive qualities, his energetic mobility and his capacity to absorb new ideas; such mobility can be looked at, somewhat whimsically, as a basic condition for freedom of thought, for what one thought and argued on one day would not determine the ideas with which one might wish to experiment on the next. Some continuity is of course necessary if one is ever to be able to realize, in any interesting way, the expressive power of any set of ideas, but it is a continuity based upon creative expression and not upon conscience, scruple, or, to pick the most barren of reasons, logical consistency.

2. Mortmere

Julian Symons, in his book *The Thirties*, gives an interesting description of the way Auden's early work was received by its first readers; in doing so, he does much to define the tantalizing and attractive atmosphere of *Poems* (1930) and *The Orators*.

It should be possible for any reader to see that Auden's *Poems* (1930) and *The Orators* (1932) belong to that small class of works which have an absolute importance and value at the time of their publication because they express cohesively a set of attitudes which have been waiting for an expositor. . . . It would be wrong to say that this feeling had no aesthetic basis, but it was not primarily aesthetic. What one felt, as nearly as such things can be put into crude words, was: 'Here is somebody who expresses what I believe myself, but have never been able to say.' The atmosphere of schoolboy plotting, the heartiness, the assonances and half-rhymes, all these were wonderfully refreshing after the dryness of Eliot and his imitators; the frequent references to science and psychoanalysis found a response in our vague awareness of these things; and,

pushing deeper, there was something profoundly congenial in Auden's idea that 'love' was not adequate in
itself, was even somehow wrong.[1]

As this summary indicates, the special atmosphere of
Auden's early poetry depends on a number of qualities,
both literary and extra-literary; insofar as Auden's poetry
embodied certain tones of voice and attitudes common to
his generation, it became a rallying point and, by extension,
a sign of a kind of liberation of mind. The nature of this
liberation is, however, difficult to determine. A preliminary
step toward understanding it is provided by a comparison
of Auden's early work with the products of the Surrealist
movement in France in the previous decade. Although both
Auden and the Surrealists were dedicated to exposing the
moribund character of contemporary society and although
both at times either collaborated with the Communist party
or espoused the Marxist view of history, considerable differences remained between them in both political attitude
and poetic style. The Surrealists strove toward a " 'revolution' in experience to be brought about by the mind and
the imagination once the fetters of rationalism and habit
had been struck off. Aragon challenged his audience in
Madrid: do you believe, yes or no, in the infinite powers of
thought? We will prevail against all odds."[2] Auden, however close to absurdity his early and highly fertile fantasy
brought him, never wanted to strike off the "fetters of

[1] London: Cresset Press, 1960, pp. 14–15.

[2] Robert S. Short, "The Politics of Surrealism," in *Leftwing Intellectuals between the Wars*, ed. Walter Laqueur and George
Mosse (New York: Harper and Row, 1966), p. 5.

rationalism" but rather to use ideas and his rational imagination in a new way, at his most extreme exploring parody and contradiction for their own sakes. Similarly, Auden's occasional indulgence in attitudes that seem to reveal a belief in "the infinite powers of thought" remains much qualified by the tone of the verse.

A more adequate definition of the tendentious aspects of Auden's early poetry can be approached through one of the qualities pointed out by Symons, "the atmosphere of schoolboy plotting." Criticism of the English public-school system, as has often been noted in connection with Auden, plays a great part in the early poetry. Far more important than any substantive critique of the schools and, by implication, of the society that fostered them, is Auden's use of the schoolboy atmosphere and a form of fantasy closely related to it; these factors are most responsible for the particular tendentiousness of the early works (up to *Look, Stranger!*), and they serve to form a complex and not unsuccessful poetic identity. Some concrete examples of forms of tendentious language that occur in the early poetry will be helpful as starting points. In "Get there if you can and see the land you were once proud to own," Auden concludes with the oft-quoted lines:

> Drop those priggish ways for ever, stop behaving
>   like a stone:
> Throw those bath-chairs right away, and learn to
>   leave ourselves alone.
>
> If we really want to live, we'd better start at once
>   to try;

> If we don't, it doesn't matter, but we'd better start
> to die.[3]

These lines, like the poem they come from, are a bizarre mixture of analysis, denunciation, parody, didactic commentary, and high spirits. The vigor and belligerency of the tone, the qualities that make the poem tendentious, are all rooted in a kind of schoolboy exuberance; potentially serious social analysis, as in the beginning, explodes into nonsense in the list of betrayers, and, in the lines quoted above, is reduced to an intentionally adolescent standard of judgment, that is, whether one is a prig or not. The society, the speaker, and the denunciation itself are all made fun of, and the meter is a parody of the really stuffy, the Victorians, the Tennyson of "Locksley Hall." The parody of Tennyson and, by implication, of the belief in progress to which his society subscribed (emphasized in "Locksley Hall") is not meant seriously to serve a political point (as is, for example, Bertolt Brecht's parody of Goethe in "Liturgie vom Hauch"); rather it resembles the vigorous and extravagant gesture of an *enfant terrible* who is also a naughty boy.

A different kind of example is provided by the poem "Consider this and in our time." Although often comic in the richness of its fantasy and although its analysis of the forces at work in the coming destruction of civilization is not altogether clear, the poem attains considerable eloquence in condemning its civilization and does not undercut that condemnation quite so obviously as does "Get there if you can." On the surface its voice seems distinctly

[3] *Poems* (London: Faber and Faber, 1930), p. 70.

different from the infantile one of the first poem; it is, however, connected with the schoolboy world in another way.
The lines that Auden later omitted show that the poem is
rooted in the early myth of an enemy that is the schoolboy's villain; the poem is leveled at the

> Financier, leaving your little room
> Where the money is made but not spent,
> You'll need your typist and your boy no more;
> The game is up for you and for the others,
> Who, thinking, pace in slippers on the lawns
> Of College Quad and Cathedral Close,
> Who are born nurses, who live in shorts
> Sleeping with people and playing fives.[4]

The villains are, as are other of the poem's figures, openly
caricatures; sometimes Auden's caricature types, portrayed
with a kind of viciousness, approach the drawings of George
Grosz, in which capitalists with varicose veins wander in a
world of psychological and social degeneration, violence,
prostitution, and unspeakably pernicious dachshunds. The
caricature of these poetic lines is less concentrated than
that of Grosz; it is a mixture of many criteria of judgment,
more or less fantastic, and, in singling out the college don
as victim, it breaks into a world where the villains themselves are absurd and therefore, in a certain sense, unreal.
The caricature is, in short, more nonsensical than it is ma-
licious. The financier is partly condemned on the basis of
the Marxist analysis of the exploitative manipulation of
capital and partly exposed as a decadent and exploitative
homosexual; the former has some political impact, but the

4 Ibid., p. 78.

latter is sheer comic abuse with none of the grotesque detail of a Grosz prostitute. The college don is completely fantastic as a villain, even though Auden is using him in part to criticize the sickness and triviality of unengaged thought; the unmanly and ludicrous don is too large a target to be much more than an absurd straw man, and the fact that he is such an easy target makes the act of knocking him down all the more fun.

In Auden's early poetry, then, the political element is subordinate to comic fantasy, and it becomes crucial to an understanding of the tendency of the poems to examine in detail the nature of this fantasy. The first aspect to underline is the importance of fads to Auden's imagination; from this standpoint, new light can be shed upon the nature of literary influence on Auden. Auden was, according to both Isherwood and Spender, a creature of changing and extravagantly asserted enthusiasms, a characteristic that smacks very much of the schoolboy. Isherwood reports Auden's passing infatuation with Emily Dickinson, and he also notes that Auden, every time one met him, had a new and faddish word with which to judge everything; likewise, the story of Auden's various and vehement opinions about the novels of Ronald Firbank is recorded by Spender. The effects of such conscious faddishness are not hard to discern. First, it allows the writer a freedom of experiment far greater than if he remained serious or tried to keep to material and modes of expression that he could intellectually *and* emotionally absorb. One can play at being Emily Dickinson, use her tight metrics and epigrammatic style without having to compare himself seriously to her, and one can do so with the additional, mainly private enjoyment of the game.

Second, such faddishness can itself generate a poetic personality, a style and mode of speech particularly amusing to those who are in on the game and with a certain rhetorical range.

The most interesting description of this aspect of Auden's nature is Spender's; Auden's prose and conversation was filled with strictures that were here today and gone tomorrow and that he pronounced in an ironic, self-conscious manner, as if each phrase should be enclosed by quotation marks.

> 'Those who believe that there is anything valuable in our youth as such we have neither the patience to consider nor the power to condone: our youth should be a period of spiritual discipline, not a self-justifying dogma. As for the intelligent reader, we can only remind him, when he experiences distaste, that no universalized system—political, religious, or metaphysical —has been bequeathed to us: where pleasure, that it is but an infinitesimal progression towards a new synthesis—one more of those efforts as yet so conpicuous in their paucity.'

> This mixture of the austere with the extravagant, the kind of burlesque and self-mockery, the pleasure is abstract phraseology mouthed so as to suggest a kind of incantation, in this passage, recall Auden's conversation. 'So conspicuous in their paucity,' I can imagine him saying with an upwards jerking movement of his head. He would hold the vowels between the consonants as though in steel forceps.[5]

[5] *World within World* (London: Hamish Hamilton, 1951), p. 57.

The self-mockery and burlesque are those of an adult consciousness indulging itself in the childish pleasure of trying on modes of language and ideas that are too big, that are themselves pretentious and not seriously held—and almost getting away with it. Such experimental burlesque was perhaps inevitable for a sensitive child in the English public-school system, living apart from his family in an ingrown, highly intellectualized bastion of Georgian tradition. The experience of Cyril Connolly provides an interesting example; he writes of the way in which learning beyond the emotional range of a young boy was transformed by the boy into a kind of role model:

> We were both absorbed in Renaissance history and translated everything we learnt into our own lives; after reading Machiavelli I practiced Machiavellianism, drawing up analyses of whom I should sit next, whom make friends with; of how to separate So-and-so, how to win over someone else.[6]

It would be difficult indeed to look back, without an urge to parody, upon a tradition that was first absorbed in this manner, presented in an environment that attempted to weld together the discordant elements of wide reading in an intensely aesthetic atmosphere with the rituals and sentiments of a boys' school. The temptation to misuse humorously this literary tradition, the act of a kind of literary maverick, would be strong; one thinks of the transmutation of Wilfred Owen and Katherine Mansfield into the familiar gods, Wilfred and Kathy. Dante in the mouth of an absurd schoolmaster, a landscape of decay turned farce, and Law-

[6] *Enemies of Promise* (Boston: Little, Brown, 1939), p. 262.

rence and Baudelaire played off against Ludendorff are all examples of this, more or less extreme.

Some of the catchwords of Auden criticism can be reinterpreted in a similar manner; they are strictures made in a tone of voice conscious of its own pretentiousness and modishness. Although the phrase "clinical detachment" is an apt term for the discussion of Auden's work, it is not only that. Like the phrase "conspicuous in their paucity," it would have been uttered by Auden in a particular manner; the sentence in which, according to Spender, Auden used the phrase gives us an indication of the kind of overtones it carried. "A poet must be clinical, dispassionate about life. The poet feels much less strongly about these things than do other people."[7] Clearly these words are not intended simply and seriously as either a kind of poetic platform or as a description of what Auden intends for himself. He is highly conscious of himself playing—in a slightly clowning fashion—the role of Grounder of New Poetic Style; the audacity and the slightly pedantic character of the second sentence has about it a touch of the joker, the person on to the literary game of platforms and movements and bright new emergent talents. There is also an aura of the mock-elegant in-joke about such pronouncements; they are made to the small coterie of Auden's followers at Oxford, a group very conscious of its exclusiveness and private ritual, and one which Auden dominated, choosing those who were to be admitted and naming them *the* modern novelist or *the* dramatist of the future.

[7] "W. H. Auden and His Poetry," in *Auden: A Collection of Critical Essays*, ed. Monroe Spears (Englewood Cliffs, N.J.: Prentice Hall, 1964), p. 27.

This atmosphere of latent buffoonery, humorously elegant ritual, and in-joke is of far more than incidental importance to Auden's poetic beliefs. Auden characteristically seizes upon ideas and dogmas that are themselves a bit absurd and/or modish, or, if not absurd of themselves, at least susceptible to varied—often comic—treatment. Auden's "belief" in the faith healing of John Layard and Homer Lane is the best example of this; as can be seen by Auden's use of it in analyzing his friends, it is a doctrine that allows a great deal of fanciful elaboration and is more than a little crackpot in character. Nevertheless, Auden and his friends did act upon it at times with the display of utmost seriousness; the doctrine that no disease can affect the pure in heart did, after all, cause Isherwood severe dental problems. Nor are Auden's other "beliefs," the more reputable doctrines of Marx, Freud, and Kierkegaard, free of a touch of this susceptibility to fanciful elaboration; all offer certain room for play, that of a system of belief that embodies skepticism of the absolute validity of language and ideas. Moreover, Auden exhibited his beliefs in ways that suggest that the game and rites of believing were for him a good part of the entertainment in and motivation for the belief; Auden would, in a book review, demand with "Comrade" Nemilov an ideology of sex, and the cross on the mantelpiece of his New York apartment in the forties had, as Spender describes it, more than a touch of theater to it. It is hard to believe that Auden, who at an early age had such a sense of jargon, would have abandoned it in dealing with philosophies that cultivate an abundance of specialized language along with their systems of thought. When one regards Auden and his "answers" in this light, the puzzling fact that Spender notes, that Auden has so often changed his beliefs but has so little changed his personality or style of life, becomes easier to understand; each of these beliefs is held in something of the same consciously fanciful fashion.

In order to understand the kind of mind that involves itself so much in fantasy, jargon, and faddishness, it is important to go back a step and consider what Justin Replogle calls the "gang myth," the body of fantasy built up about the Mortmere stories. Analysis of the genesis and the nature of the group myth must rely on Isherwood's *Lions and Shadows*, the only account of these fantasies that is more than cursory in nature; it deals at greatest length with the fantasy world constructed by Isherwood and Upward, but Auden came to share in these fantasies as well. Upon becoming friends with Auden, Isherwood writes, he began with him a fantasy world similar to that constructed with Upward, which had been based on their school experiences; later Auden must have come to share directly in the Mortmere world as well, for he was also a friend of Upward, and there are many traces of Mortmere in his work.

The origin of the fantasies is in a peculiar kind of personal relationship. In their ordinary life, Isherwood and Upward cultivated a kind of private language:

> People frequently said to me: "I saw you and Chalmers [Upward] in the street this morning. What on earth was the joke?" For, when we were seen together, we were always laughing. The mere tones of Chalmers' voice would start me giggling in anticipation, and I had only to pronounce some quite ordinary word

with special emphasis in order to send him into fits. We were each other's ideal audience; nothing, not the slightest innuendo or the subtlest shade of meaning, was lost between us. A joke which, if I had been speaking to a stranger, would have taken five minutes to lead up to and elaborate and explain, could be conveyed to Chalmers by the faintest hint. In fact, there existed between us that semi-telepathic relationship which connects a crossword puzzle-setter with his most expert solvers. Our conversation would have been hardly intelligible to anyone who had happened to overhear it; it was a rigamarole of private slang, deliberate misquotations, bad puns, bits of parody, and preparatory school smut.[8]

The description is interesting for a number of reasons; most striking is the blend of the aesthetic cultivation of language and the juvenile end toward which it leads, the exquisite private innuendo which elicits a giggle. On the one hand, a consciously literary relationship is thus formed; he and Upward act as each other's perfect audience more than as companions or serious friends, modes of expression are cultivated for their own sake, and conversation depends a great deal on the private use of literary reference. On the other hand, the complexities of this aesthetic posture are all built around buffoonery and the private joke.

The psychology behind the attraction to such conversation is also striking and has, no doubt, a great deal to do with the psychology of the literary homosexual of this pe-

[8] Isherwood, *Lions and Shadows* (Norfolk: New Directions, 1947), p. 65.

riod. Such talk would bind people together privately and give them the illusion of great intimacy; at the same time there would be no serious threat in the considerable emotional indulgence it provides, for the jokes and the cultivated ironic pose guard against sentiment and serious personal revelation. Once someone begins talking like this, all language is swallowed up into the irony and the special intonations. From other parts of *Lions and Shadows* we can see how such a defense was felt to be necessary; behind Isherwood's public composure and wit lies another self, one that is victim to heroic and romantic dreams that are not controlled by any sense of irony and that are felt to be not only foolish but also dangerous. After Isherwood describes a trip he made back to his old school that represented an indulgence of these fantasies, he remarks, in what is a surprising lapse in the lightness of his tone, that

> The reality was lost in the dream. It is so very easy, in the mature calm of a library, to sneer at all this homosexual romanticism. But the rulers of Fascist states do not sneer—they profoundly understand and make use of just these fantasies and longings. I wonder how, at this period, I should have reacted to the preaching of an English Fascist leader clever enough to serve up his "message" in a suitably disguised and palatable form? He would have converted me, I think, inside half an hour—provided always that Chalmers hadn't been there to interfere.[9]

Here is the more threatening side to the schoolboy world, and, although a reader might doubt that Isherwood would

[9] Ibid., pp. 78–79.

ever have been converted, it is probably true that some latent public-school homosexuality did add to the appeal of fascism, with its combination of male comraderie and strictness of discipline.

For those who felt themselves isolated from the "hearties" and the grotesque world of their normal emotions, be it through overt homosexuality, lack of skill at sports, or having been sickly and bullied as a child, the development of an opposite and ironically self-conscious fantasy world would be a weapon of sorts, as well as being a defensive, even escapist measure. The Mortmere world constructed by Isherwood and Upward exhibited certain aggressive strategies which are especially interesting in an examination of Auden's early, more socially tendentious verse. Most clearly, the fantasies acted as a form of subversion; just as the special intonation and cultivated tone of voice subverted language, so did the content of the fantasies undermine the world in which Isherwood and Upward lived. The two revenged themselves on the college, the "Poshocracy," and the dons by making them unreal; once this had been done, the transformed dons could serve as characters in fantasies spun endlessly and with the utmost absorption. The world thus transformed must from the start be something a bit fantastic; its subversion was an enthusiastic game, and one does not play thus with anything seriously hostile. The ideal subversion of reality took place when reality seemed to play along with the game, by providing Isherwood and Upward with material that fit:

> Our conception of "the Combine" and our burlesque cult of the Sinister coloured the most trivial incidents

of our everyday life. We were psychic tourists, setting out to discover a metaphysical University City.
Everywhere, we encountered enemy agents. We recognized them instantly, by the discreetly threatening
tones of their voices. One afternoon, I was buying
some clothes at a draper's. "This tie's rather nicer," I
said. And the shopman, with what we later described
as a "reptilian sneer," answered smilingly: "Yes—
they're *all* rather nicer. . . ." There was a college
waiter who murmured into one's ear, as he took the
order: "Most *certainly* sir." This man seemed posi-
tively fiend-like: he surely must be an important spy.[10]

In this sort of subversion, no one is seriously harmed and
no one earnestly threatened; it is a "burlesque cult" that
thrives on the consciousness of its own burlesque. It is,
moreover, profoundly self-indulgent; it allows the mind a
form of uninhibited and effortless play apart from all outside criticism, for, as Isherwood writes, they never really
wanted to write down the Mortmere adventures as stories,
because that would be to deprive them of the game itself,
that of drawing the Mortmere setting out into ever more
complicated whimsies. Also, since Isherwood and Upward
were conscious of themselves as aspiring writers, the fantasies brought with them the additional pleasure that one has
when feeling his own inventiveness; it makes one believe
for a while that he is creative and imaginative.

A second aspect of the Mortmere world is the complement to its subversive tendency; the fantasies also represent
a comic form of magical control of a "hostile" environ-

[10] Ibid., p. 67.

ment. Although the Mortmere world was one of the spy and the secret agent, the trained betrayers, its creators were in control of everything that happened within it and, since Mortmere had roots in the lives they were then leading, by extension they would come jokingly to imagine themselves as able to control Cambridge as well through their fantasies. Several examples of this occur in *Lions and Shadows*. Through a kind of poetic imagery, for example, revenge was to be had:

> If we pretended to believe that Laily [an imaginary don] and his colleagues were plotting day and night against us, we said also that, very soon, the powers of the [Rat's] Hostel would counter-attack. Chalmers made a ballad which began:
>> About the middle of the night, a Thing with fins
>> Came to reprove the Tutor for his sins . . .
> (The rest, unfortunately, is not printable).[11]

They also looked forward to the apocalyptic moment when the fantasies would be realized in the real world of Cambridge:

> At the end of that term, there was a college feast. Chalmers and I had looked forward to this ceremony for some time; it promised to be a suitable opportunity for an overt act of hostility to the "Other Side." Exactly what we were going to do, we didn't know. Perhaps Chalmers would simply jump on the table and shout: "*J'en appelle!*"—whereupon, we said, the earth would open and the dons, the silver heirloom plate and

[11] Ibid., p. 72.

the college buildings themselves would be immediately engulfed. The phrase "*J'en appelle!*", which occurs in a poem by Villon, meant, in our private slang, a kind of metaphysical challenge. Just as when, in poker, one says: "I'll see you!" We challenged the "Other Side" to show us their cards. They dreaded this challenge because, of course, they had been bluffing. Once the bluff had been called, we liked to imagine, the entire acadmic "blague" became bankrupt and would automatically collapse.

Needless to say, what really happened was that we had an excellent dinner and that I got drunk.[12]

By now a number of ideas that seem also very relevant to Auden and his early work have been touched upon; Auden is the writer who turned this fantasy world most successfully to concrete literary use. Before returning to a consideration of Auden's work, we should investigate more generally what is involved in turning this fantasy into literature, just what rhetorical possibilities it affords and what difficulties are involved. Both Isherwood and Upward had grappled with bringing this essentially private material into the public domain; they attempted several times to write stories based on the Mortmere world. Isherwood gave up; his Berlin stories are just the opposite of Mortmere, realistic tales of people he knew, in which he remains for the most part in the background, serving only as narrator. Upward was unable to abandon the fantasies; his only successful use of that world was the story "The Railroad Accident," an amusing and sometimes Kafkaesque description of a

---

[12] Ibid., pp. 114–115.

race to a party, a train wreck, a treasure hunt, and finally a
duel, the whole of which may or may not be real and is
part nightmare, part parody. The problem for Upward
was to make these fantasies substantial enough to be interesting to a general public. One solution was to write a kind
of dream literature, which, although any event, no matter
how fantastic, may take place, has a sense of nonlogical
necessity to it; "The Railroad Accident," with the perva-
sive suggestion of a sinister plot and sudden violence, all of
which may well be a creation of the narrator's own mind,
is an excellent example of this solution. Another is that to
which Upward came later in his career; one can dramatize
the fantasies purely as creations of the narrator's disordered
mind and use as plot the events that bring him gradually
back into touch with reality. This possibility was used for
the structure of *Journey to the Border*, where a fantasy-
ridden schoolmaster is gradually converted to Marxism;
the story's moralizing and the schoolmaster's unbelievably
hysterical mind make it a failure, and one is very aware of
Upward's private axe-grinding, his need to find some use
for the Mortmere world and his desire to affirm Marxist
dogma. A third possibility also exists; one can, as did Rex
Warner in *The Wild Goose Chase*, control the fantasy material by means of an allegorical structure; Warner's allegory of the grounding of a new, basically Marxist future,
however, reveals itself as mechanical as soon as one becomes
aware of its simplicity and patness.

All of these possibilities are realized in one form or another in Auden's early poetry and in many cases quite successfully. The construction of a world in which dream
logic is the guiding principle, the unreliable neurotic

speaker, and an allegorical structure for the poetry are critical commonplaces, and one can often observe all three things at work in a single poem. The important question, however, remains: just why did Auden succeed where others had failed?

A number of reasons can be found. The most important is that, for reasons of temperament, Auden would not have been involved in the fantasies in the way that Isherwood was. For Isherwood the fantasies were a form of imagination that defended him against and liberated him from a dangerous kind of romantic sentiment; by contrast, Auden was notable for his lack of feelings of guilt, inadequacy, and secret fears from which such sentiment sprang. According to Isherwood, Auden was not embarrassed by personal topics; neither was he hesitant to talk with Isherwood about his frank and voracious sexual appetite, nor did he refrain from commenting on things personally embarrassing to Isherwood. Moreover, Auden used this "clinical detachment" to control his friends: "He had already an extensive knowledge of the theories of modern psychology, which he used as a means of understanding himself and dominating his friends."[13] Auden's self-confidence and peculiarly independent and effective use of his intelligence are his most outstanding qualities:

> For his Oxford contemporaries the most impressive thing about Auden undoubtedly was that, at such an early age, he was so confident and conscious a master of his situation. Not only did he hold very definite views about literature, but he also had a philosophy

[13] Spender, p. 54.

of life which, if juvenile, at least explained to him
his own actions and those of his friends. . . . His aims
were to fulfill his potentialities, obtain satisfaction for
his desires, and maintain his attitudes, without prejudice and without accepting any authority outside his
own judgment. At the same time he avoided coming
into unnecessary conflict with the interests and views
of those around him. As a youth he was outrageous,
but he was not a rebel. His clinical view of living,
whereby he regarded life as an operation performed
by a surgically minded individual upon the carefully
analysed and examined body and soul of the society
around him, was amoral. . . . The only generally accepted virtue which he himself accepted was courage,
because courage was required by anyone wishing to
achieve his own independent development.[14]

This picture of Auden is no doubt a highly idealized one;
Spender's own avowed insecurities seem to find their complement in the emotional and intellectual self-possession of
Auden. But Auden's dominance among his friends seems
to have been based in large part upon this very image, his
ability to use whatever philosophy he then professed to
explain himself and dominate others: he was so easy in this
role that he could practice it with detachment and with a
rhetorical range that stretched from buffoonery to a kind
of a comic grandeur. He was quite conscious of pleasing
his audience in doing so—indeed, he tried, according to
both Isherwood and Spender, to be a success on family

[14] Ibid., p. 53.

visits; it was this desire and ability to please that made others willingly accept his intellectual domination.

A second and equally important factor of temperament was responsible for Auden's success in using the Mortmere world, and it explains as much as the far more famous "clinical detachment" some of the distinctive quality of Auden's verse. As Isherwood repeatedly notes, the Mortmere world was an escapist world, both in its fantasy content and in the way in which its creators participated; whereas Isherwood and Upward seemed to have considerable difficulties in accepting emotionally the escapism and self-indulgence, Auden seems to have had none. As a child, Auden had built for himself a private fantasy world that was avowedly escapist and self-indulgent, but that kept these tendencies under a kind of prosaic arbitrary control by means of certain rules:

> Neither Mr. Woolf nor Mr. Waugh seems to have indulged in a kind of daydreaming that was of immense importance to my childhood. Between the ages of six and twelve, I spent a great many of my waking hours in the construction and elaboration of a private sacred world, the basic elements of which were a landscape, northern and limestone, and an industry, lead mining. In constructing it, fantasy had to submit to two rules. In deciding what objects were to be included, I was free to select this and reject that, on condition that both were real objects (two kinds of water turbine, for instance, which could be found in textbooks on mining machinery or a manufacturer's catalogue); I was not allowed to invent one. In deciding how my

> world was to function, I could choose between two
> practical possibilities (a mine could be drained either
> by an adit or by a pump), but physical impossibilities
> and magic means were forbidden.[15]

Also, the image that Auden presents of himself is often one
of an almost elegant capacity for self-indulgence. One
notes it in gestures recorded by Isherwood, such as select-
ing the largest cigar on an after-dinner platter; it is implicit
in Auden's mode of speech, the way he pronounced each
word with a relish for its sound and connotation; and it
comes out directly in a number of the poems, both in style
—in the way Auden is conscious of sound and literary effect—and in theme, in such poems as those based on one of
his favorite poetic settings, the sea resort. Generally, a form
of self-indulgence lies behind every attitude that is held
and used for the sake of its rhetoric and with the consciousness of this use; paradoxically, then, the idea of "clinical
detachment" itself must be seen as a form of self-indulgence: in applying it to himself, Auden is enjoying the role
of Grounder of New Poetic Style which it entails.

Auden's success with the materials of Mortmere rests
finally on his ability to use with gusto, finesse, and literary
tact the rhetorical possibilities that world provided; at the
heart of Auden's work there is an enjoyment of rhetoric
and the rules of rhetoric for their own sakes, an inclination
toward a kind of baroque riddling, fantastic eloquence, and
a love for the word and thought made rich by innuendo
and outside reference, be it private or public. Probably the

[15] "As It Seemed to Us," *The New Yorker*, 41 (April 3, 1965),
169–170.

clearest example would be the "Journal of an Airman";
Auden's use of his sources was based on his attempt to ex-
ploit both their inherent rhetorical possibilities and those
made available by combining them. One finds a comparable
interest in rhetorical effect in the *Poems:* a consideration of
the most substantial and politically tendentious poems of
Auden's first volume indicates how important it is to be
conscious of their rhetoric as such and, along with this,
how such rhetoric becomes tendentious.

The predominantly serious tone of "It was Easter as I
walked in the public gardens" seems to belie this view.[16]
The opening, for example, is a highly conscious setting of
moods. There is the freshness of rediscovery in the "emphasis on new names, on the arm / A fresh hand with
fresh power"; there is a depth of pity in the grotesque discovery of "solitary man" as "Helpless and ugly as an em-
bryo chicken"; there is resolution in the gratuitous beauty
and refreshment of the "sudden shower"; and throughout
there is an atmosphere of extended and sympathetic contemplation. The general progress of the poem represents
a gradual deepening of this contemplation; the second section begins with an abstraction applied to the present scene,
which extends itself into first a bitter memory and then a
more purely abstract meditation; and the third section, describing a trip to a country cottage juxtaposed with a meditation about a return to childhood and origins, continues
this process, until resolution is found first in the abstraction
of being "weaned at last to independent delight" and then
in the wider vision ushered in by the "violent laugh of a

[16] *Poems,* pp. 55–61.

jay," a reminder from his environment to leave the wood and look about him.

There is, however, something extremely stagey about Auden's setting of mood, particularly at the beginning of the poem, and throughout the interplay between thought and present setting begins to seem stage-managed. Of course, nothing is wrong with or particularly unusual about such stage-managing—Auden constantly does it; what becomes distinctive is the way the stage-management is used and the end to which it leads. This cannot be established without simultaneously evaluating the poem's quality; it is a sometimes beautiful failure, and the way in which it fails can be instructive. In general, the rhetoric seems a little flaccid; it is overworked, sometimes affected, and yet this quality of the rhetoric is not deliberate, something consciously exploited, as in a number of Auden's poems. It has none of the self-mocking irony of "Let the florid trumpet praise"; instead, the poem tries seriously to create the drama of a mind's self-exploration and this without the toughness and conscious use of rhetoric as part of the drama found in poems of Yeats. Indicative of this consciousness of rhetorical effect for its own sake is that lines like "The frozen buzzard flipped down the weir" have been salvaged from earlier poetry and pasted into this poem; what counts most is the effect of the line and not the unity of experience of the poem as a whole. The most striking evidence for this is the fact that, in the last section, Auden takes back what he has said earlier; it is as if he were conscious of having extended the rhetoric of serious and sympathetic contemplation beyond his own feeling for the subject contemplated and decides to apply to the main attitude of the poem a sudden, sharp, ironic judgment. The speaker, seemingly resolved and renewed in the previous sections, reveals that that renewal was not genuine and thus he becomes suddenly part of the death-infected gang, curable only by a revolutionary upheaval; the flaccidity of the meditation is brought to an abrupt halt with the sudden energy of "It is time for the destruction of error," a sentence unprepared for, but one that introduces the most vigorous section of the poem. Also, it is interesting to note that, in the original version of the poem, the content of the beginning was explicitly undercut by a stanza that draws too easily on T. S. Eliot:

> For this is how it ends,
> The account of growing, the history of knowing,
> As more comatose and always in,
> Living together in wretched weather
> In a doorless room in a leaking house,
> Wrong friends at the wrong time.

Thus, Auden has effected one of his notorious changes in the identity of his speaker and brought his reliability into question; the derivative nature of this repudiation indicates that the change is, as are the preceding sections, a managed effect more than anything else. Sometimes, as in "Will you turn a deaf ear," the device of the unreliable speaker produces a very interesting rhetorical effect, an atmosphere partly riddling and partly threatening. Here no such atmosphere is created, for the change is not the imperceptible shifting of values and point of view of "Will you turn a deaf ear" but rather an abrupt reversal that explodes something that seemed to take itself seriously up to the final stanza. This does not imply that for Auden the elaborate setting of mood and extended contemplation are *always* doomed to failure by their incompatibility with his sensibility; indeed, the fact that he can write the former in shorter form is well exemplified by the haunting "Doom is dark and deeper than any sea-dingle." But in "It was Easter as I walked in the public gardens" Auden has extended the mood of the beginning beyond its rhetorical limits; he has attempted to make it a unitary poetic fable and to do so is very difficult for him. For Auden successfully to extend such a poem beyond the length of something like "Doom is dark and deeper than any sea-dingle," the poem must not remain fixed in one mood, one form of rhetoric; as with Auden's later and highly successful contemplative verse, there must be great freedom for rhetorical variation. Auden's skills and inclinations are not fitted to capturing sustained emotion or sustaining dramatic structure; rather they are suited for good conversation, characterized by interesting decoration, an entertaining variety of tone, or, if the poem is comic, a wittily discordant variety of tone.

The final stanza of "It was Easter as I walked in the public gardens" seems more like Auden than the rest of the poem; the Mortmere world of deck chairs, rugger fields, and the enemy suddenly emerges, in a vigorous and fantastic evocation of "Death of the old gang." The serious meditation has ended in the absurd, intentionally contentless parody-images of the "hard bitch and the riding master" which have, despite their fantastic nature, a peculiarly enthusiastic power, indeed a greater vividness than the preceding, more carefully thought-out sections.[17]

[17] These images suggest the ruling class; and, as John Fuller

"Consider this and in our time"[18] is perhaps Auden's greatest exercise in the evocation of neurotic death, and it uses the rhetorical possibilities of the Mortmere myth fully; the Auden of 1930, when most tendentious and eloquent in describing the moribund state of his culture, relies most upon the energy and fantasy of Mortmere. The poem is not nonsense; it is based upon a fairly coherent psychological-political allegory. The depression world, one characterized by the exaggerated contrasts between the wealth of the Sport Hotel and the decay of "silted harbours" and "derelict works," breeds, through its distortions, a variety of neuroses in both those who support the system and those who are potentially treasonable to it; the destruction of this society can therefore be depicted as the action of a magically verbal Antagonist, a psychologized vision of historical necessity. But this political-psychological allegory does not account for the poem's peculiarly tendentious energy; for this, we must return to Mortmere. The poem touches most of the possibilities latent in the myth and gives them unity by means of its voice, by the sustained eloquence of the description of death; it is this tension that gives the poem its power. The landscape is a variation on Mortmere; it is one in which social detail and analysis, psychological neurosis, and high-level caricature are all inextricably blended. The caricatures that inhabit this landscape are familiar types to the Auden connoisseur: farmers in their stormy fens, the handsome and diseased youngsters, the solitary

---

suggests, the bridegroom could be a symbol of Christ. But these explanations do not touch the real source of the images' energy and suggestiveness.

[18] *Poems*, pp. 76–78.

women agents, the financiers, the dons, and the ruined boys; they are made melodramatic by being aligned with two opposed and hostile powers, the world of the dons and the world of the rat's hostel. The supreme Antagonist then emerges from this landscape and cast of characters less as an allegorical figure than as a fantastic apotheosis of the voice of the poem, bolstered by the description of him (it?) in language carrying the weight of old-Icelandic doom.

The action of the poem is also a realization of Mortmere; it brings to powerful focus a great deal of the myth's tendentiousness. The weapon of the Antagonist is one of the main staples of Mortmere: it is the "rumor, soft / But horrifying in its capacity to disgust," the sinister realization of the Mortmere cult of the innuendo, the subverting but essentially contentless statement. The effect it brings about is also Mortmerian: in part it is one of parody-horror, the appearance of a quasi-surrealistic "Thing with fins" in the chamber of the naked Don, and in part a variation on the telepathic revenge, the revenge through the word and the fantasy, which lay at the heart of the myth's construction. In general, the poem embodies both of the principal tendencies of the Mortmere world discussed above; it represents a subversion of the real world by an elaborate fantasy, and it culminates in an apocalyptic confrontation when the fantasy becomes real. This confrontation is most concretely portrayed in the lines omitted from the later versions of the poem: the financier and the don are cast out, as the poem has, so to speak, leapt to the table and *J'en appelled* them; they are then supposed to "become bankrupt and automatically collapse." The end of the poem

generalizes this effect and realizes it in terms of the Mortmere idea of flight to a psychological border; now included
in the explosion and collapse are all "seekers after happiness." The classification of the enemy in these terms is
rhetorically perfect. It names a kind of heresy that is both
psychological and social in nature; it is both a certain kind
of disease of the heart—for you are destined to "follow /
The convolutions of your simple wish"—and a characteristic of a social class, symbolized by the don and the financier, for whom the good life consists of leisure, financial
security, and finally pleasure. But while it seems to distinguish a class of individuals fated to destruction, it undercuts
these distinctions entirely and includes us all: in the Marxist sense, we of Auden's class, the class of those liable to
read poetry, are doomed to revolutionary overthrow and,
in the Freudian sense, everyone is a seeker after happiness,
for the pleasure principle operates in the consciousness of
each man, especially strongly, perhaps, in those who use
poetry to entertain themselves. The reader's world is thus
being subverted from within; while the voice of the poem
is calling for the destruction of an outside enemy, Auden
brings the reader to the discovery of the enemy within
himself, by means of the familiar technique of a distinction
that is really all-inclusive.

The description of the particular kind of fantasy that
Auden's early work represents comes back to the question posed at the beginning of this chapter: just how is
one to evaluate the tendency of such fantasy with respect
to the poetic and political upheaval of Auden's time? A
number of answers have already been suggested by the
description of the Mortmere world; now two further and

more focused kinds of answers are required. Following the conceptual division of poetic from political upheaval, the effect of Auden's poetry on poetic tradition should be considered and, for this purpose, a comparison with a different sort of aggressive and outrageous fantasy, that of Dadaism, will be made; then we will explore where such poetry fits into the political movement of the early thirties.

The Mortmere and Dada fantasies have much in common besides high spirits and propensity for nonsense. Both were creations of small, self-conscious, exuberant, and childish literary groups, who were fully aware of all the cliches and the posturing of the literary racket and who continually parodied both the racket and themselves in their roles as artists. Isherwood's statement about the Mortmere world, that it was a "parody of parody," applies equally well to Dada; not only is other literature parodied, but the very act of creation, the much publicized process of making literature, is parodied as well. A second similarity, more important for our purposes, lies in the relation of the fantasy to reality; both groups used fantasy as a chief weapon in a kind of "demolition job" on contemporary notions of culture, and by extension, the society that fostered them. To a certain extent, they had a common enemy, an unspiritual society:

> All the revolts of modern art were nothing more or less than attempts to overcome the spiritual deficiency of a previous epoch. Artistic movements from Futurism to Cubism, from Surrealism and Constructivism to abstract Expressionism (and even Pop-art today) reveal themselves as attempts to discover by various means— often with irony and pranks and sometimes with force

—a new form of spirituality or to transmit to the spectator that which art is capable of transmitting, namely transcendence, a relationship to the spiritual, an understanding of irrationality as creative power. This is certainly true, even though all this was attempted in different ways. The only artistic movement, however, that truly understood the problem was Dadaism; it did so by means of the acceptance and understanding of nothingness.[19]

More important is that the kind of fantasy that sets itself against this enemy has certain stable characteristics. The major one is, of course, the extensive and aggressive use of parody and nonsense; a second is aptly described by Michel Beaujour:

The German Dadaists, pacificists during the war found themselves at the sides of the Communists during the aborted German revolution. We aim to show that their extreme productions (that is, their most typical ones, since we are dealing after all with extremist movements) barely disguise an infatuation with edenism or apocalypse.[20]

The "infatuation with edenism or apocalypse" is similarly observable in the structure of the Mortmere fantasies. As an enclosed world, they were edenic, and they represented a form of escapist pleasure for their creators; for the Dadaists, an eden lay in the accommodation of oneself

[19] Richard Huelsenbeck, *Dada* (Hamburg: Rowohlt, 1964), p. 14. My translation.
[20] "Flight out of Time: Poetic Language and the Revolution," *Yale French Studies*, 39 (1937), 40.

in art and life to chaos, the passing moment, and the confusion of pure chance, whereas, for the Auden "gang," eden lay in the mock pastoralism of their cult of the schoolboy intrigue and villain and in a style of life in which *"Le mot juste . . .* seemed to be the solution to most of our problems."[21] The apocalypse of the Dadaists was the demolition job to be done on society, culture, and rationality, a pure act of destruction unconnected with any plan for setting something in the place of what had been destroyed, which, as such, was something consciously outrageous; Isherwood's vision of the sudden explosion of the dons and the poshocracy with one resonant *J'en appelle* is similarly outrageous and contentless.

At this point, however, the differences between the Dadaists and Auden and his friends become more significant than the similarities; Auden's "gang" was clearly much less aggressive and exuberantly revolutionary in its fantasies than were the Dadaists. Most obvious is the fact that, whereas Dada was a forceful and international literary movement, Auden and his friends were few and created essentially private fantasies, rooted in the particularly English subculture of the public school. Thus, the nonsense implicit in these fantasies had a much more restricted shock and scope than did that of the Dadaist, which was overtly and directly hostile to culture and society. Some of the early Dada performances were so tumultuous that they risked ending in bloodshed, much, of course, to the delight of the performers. According to Richard Huelsenbeck, they were intent upon striking a blow at society through the fact that Dadism "overcame not only artistic

[21] Isherwood, p. 163.

directions but also art itself, art being understood as one
of mankind's—and this time it was a mankind in need—
safety valves."[22] The fantasy of Auden and his friends was
not so directly and completely opposed to society; indeed,
there is an important sense in which it represented a
fulfillment of certain traditions and values; it was, after all,
an extension of the public-school subculture, and, in being
extravagant and idiosyncratic, it represented exactly what
one of Isherwood's masters, a prototype of the "good"
master, asked of him:

> "Not that we dislike mountains as mountains," Chal-
> mers was careful to add, "but we decline to subscribe
> to the loathsome alpine blague." ("Blague" was a
> prominent word in the new Rouen vocabulary, we
> had used it several hundred times already during the
> last forty-eight hours.) Mr. Holmes, without being
> in a position to appreciate these fine shades of disap-
> proval, was delighted. As usual, he asked nothing
> better than that we should behave with the maximum
> of eccentricity.[23]

Thus, with Auden, one often has the sense that the extravagance is exhibitionistic play which seeks approval and
secret complicity; the note is struck in such poems as "Get
there if you can," where, the voice of the precocious child
is used as social criticism at the same time that its energy
and nonsense invite amused participation and approval,
even when it puts us in the category of those who haven't
learned "to leave ourselves alone."

[22] Huelsenbeck, p. 13. My translation.
[23] Isherwood, p. 32.

The ways in which Auden's poetry acts in complicity with English society and literary tradition are noted by Randall Jarrell in his brilliant though mistaken article "Freud to Paul: The Stages of Auden's Ideology." Jarrell argues that "Auden is managing to stay on surprisingly good terms with Authority by assuming the role of *enfant terrible* of the reformers—a very goodhearted and very childish one, the *enfant terrible* of the old father's long soft summer dreams."[24] The argument that Jarrell has built around this observation—that Auden is driven by the guilt which his rebellion raises in him to ultimately embrace the authority he apparently rejects—is finally misleading; not only does it ascribe an intense and personal sense of guilt to someone who seems remarkably free from it, someone who, though he recurs time and time again to the word, does so in such a cheery, exuberant, and confident manner that the word seems more an abstraction than a felt reality, but also it attempts to psychoanalytically "one-up" someone who has, himself, a thorough knowledge of psychoanalysis and of the particular mechanism Jarrell is referring to. What is much more likely is that Auden is well aware of the ways in which guilty rebellion tends to lead to submission to authority and is using this insight, playfully, as one of the chief ideas of his early poems; in doing so, he becomes an *enfant terrible* of an unusually conscious sort, one whose rebelliousness does not consist of self-deceptive attempts to seriously unseat an authority-figure or a social order, but rather of the engaging, semi-bohemian self-indulgence of someone who plays with ideas

[24] *Partisan Review*, 12 (1945), 449.

that "responsible" people—a group that includes the Jarrell of this essay—would like to take seriously. As such, Auden is even more the *"enfant terrible* of the old father's long soft dreams" than Jarrell makes him out to be; he is not only the one who flirts with ideas of rebellion and renewal, but he is also the one who gracefully and wittily escapes having to take even these things wholly seriously, the one who, by his grace and virtuosic wit, remains essentially innocent, even during the most ardent disquisitions on guilt. If anything, then, Auden's later "conversion" to existentialist Christianity is not a submission to authority, but the acquisition of an authority that allows a more inclusive and congenial arena for essential playfulness; in Auden's most successful religious poems, the authority figure, a God approachable only through fear and trembling, remains just outside the limits of an explicitly secular verse, one that can include a greater range of social characters and ideas than ever before, and one that retains—though in a more mature, sophisticated form—its maverick comic extravagance, as if confident of divine approval for this least of all possible human wickednesses.

A far more concrete difference between the Dadaists and the Auden "gang" lies in the fact that the Dadaists in their lives and literary experiments "were creative irrationalists, because we had understood, unconsciously much more than consciously, the sense of chaos."[25] The Dadaists attempted to destroy language, its meaning, and all traditional notions of literature based on this meaning, and their weapons ranged from parody to the adoption of literary forms that made nonsense of the idea of literary

[25] Huelsenbeck, p. 10. My translation.

form, such as the sound poem, the simultaneous poem, and the static poem. With Auden the case was very different; he wrote within traditional forms, often subverting them slightly or robbing them of all earnestness by playing with them, but never attempting to explode the notion of literary form itself. The nonsense of the Mortmere world is not really hostile to the English literary tradition; it is, in its creation of a separate fantasy world for the sake of amusement with an escapist tinge, very close to the work of Lewis Carroll and Edward Lear. Carroll's logical games, for example, are quite similar to Auden's love of the absurd riddle; and the notion of nonsense as a collection of discordant pieces in which there is "no fusion and synthesis, no calling in of the dream faculty to lend the whole so formed new significances beyond logic"[26] could easily be applied to *The Orators*.

The most interesting distinction between Dada and the fantasies of Auden and his friends can be seen by looking at the effect each wished to have. Dada, like its name, "means nothing. This is the meaningful nothingness, in which nothing means something. We want to change the world with nothing, we want to change writing and painting with nothing, and we want to end the war with nothing."[27] The statement is at once its own parody; it parodies the idea of poetic-political platforms in that it makes use of absurd paradox, implicit in which is the reminder that Dada is itself a hoax, as the arbitrariness and

[26] Elizabeth Sewell, *The Field of Nonsense* (London: Chatto and Windus, 1952), p. 98.

[27] Huelsenbeck, "Erklärung, vorgetragen im Cabaret Voltaire, im Frühjahr 1916," *Dada,* p. 30. My translation.

meaninglessness of the name suggest. The paradox and parody are ambitious and sweeping; they make nothingness, *das Nichts*, into a substantive, active principle, at the same time that it remains contentless, absurd, and fake. Auden never goes to this extreme. On the contrary, as Spender puts it, he has held throughout his life a variety of beliefs which he uses as "answers" to the questions he poses. With Auden, the Dadaistic sense of *das Nichts* comes in only through a back door: these "answers" have an effect similar to the dadaistic *Nichts* insofar as they are played with, easily changed, and only, it seems, provisionally believed in. For the poetry they provide allegorical structures, but one feels that these structures are at the same time more than a little arbitrary, and one is not very surprised when, as in "It was Easter as I walked in the public gardens," the main content of a poem is negated by a later statement, or when, as in "Consider this and in our time," the allegory is far from clear, because the psychological and the social are so fantastically intermingled and because the poem contains a number of either private or seemingly arbitrary elements.

The conclusion to which we must come, then, is that, although Auden's voice was radically new for English poetry and achieved a great notoriety among a small group of intellectuals, it never possessed the revolutionary force and intention of the continental avant-garde movements; its novelty was indeed often exhibitionistic and tendentious, but it did not represent any organized assault on literary tradition nor did Auden ever try very hard during this time to present himself as a revolutionary activist. He was now and then politically aggressive in his book reviews, condemning society and often calling, in a kind of Party voice, for change; but book reviews are a pathetic little garden plot for the revolution, and Auden's tone, even at its most aggressive, was something more like buffoonery than serious commitment: "Dearie, you can't do anything for the children until you've done something for the grown-ups."[28]

To a certain extent, Auden's early work is avant-garde, in that it represented a consciously modern and novel form of poetic language. It did oppose a disruptive and often nonsenical fantasy to conventional social and private realities; it introduced a radically new body of material into English poetry, ranging from public-school matter to private material brought consciously and aggressively into the public eye to psychoanalysis; it made new and full use of the ironies of the author's detachment from the poem; and there is a sense in which, through its parodying and plundering of tradition and through its combining of traditional aesthetic material with the schoolboy's trick of treating experience as a joke, it accomplished what Walter Benjamin claims for Dada, namely "to test the authenticity of art."[29] Above all, much of Auden's early work represented, as did Dada, a release of enthusiasm, and, despite all the ironies of decay and prophecies about the death of the old gang, the verse is anything but tired and depressed; a great deal of energy is generated and released in transmuting reality into outrageous fiction in the discovery of enemies to be destroyed by a well-aimed *mot juste*.

[28] "Private Pleasure," *Scrutiny*, 1 (1932), 194.
[29] "Der Autor als Produzent," in *Versuche über Brecht* (Frankfurt on the Main: Suhrkamp, 1966), p. 106.

It should be easy now to turn to the discussion of the relationship of Auden's poetry to the politics of the early thirties; his early work in Julian Symons' words, expressed "cohesively a set of attitudes which have been waiting for an expositor."[30] The most striking of these attitudes would be Mortmere's idea of the enemy; on the one hand, the enemy is the rigid society, repressive of the emotional greatness of D. H. Lawrence, and in this respect it is akin to the Mortmere myth written as a psychological melodrama. On the other hand, latent in the Mortmere notion of an enemy is the idea that the individual is up against a "combine," one that works against him in secret and devious ways, both through overt action and psychological conditioning, both from without and within. From here it is but a short step to a kind of psychologized Marxist version of the world where the individual confronts a threatening and repressive reality, one that has no face, but is rather the product of a system that can be only approximately identified with a certain class of individuals and exists as a psychologically malevolent force within those who are not of the proletariat. As a result, the neurosis of the Airman represents a playful variation on genuine political anxieties of many Auden's contemporaries; the most harmless of objects or customs can be aids to the enemy.

A second shared attitude would be the enthusiasm of Auden's verse, the fact that it liberates a great deal of energy in the reader. This energy corresponds to an optimism which later found expression in the political speculation of the mid-thirties; despite the fact that Auden and his readers felt that the traditional culture was bankrupt

[30] Symons, p. 14.

and moribund, their reaction was not one of Eliotic depression and despair. Instead, they felt themselves to be possessed of all the possibilities implicit in those times that seem to be turning points in history, when the future is to be grounded anew, and thus a young, energetic, and politically tendentious poetic voice could not help becoming a rallying point. Auden's particular facility with language, ideas, and startling epithets would be especially important in this respect; the way Auden was able to turn hitherto unpoetic material into poetry, seemingly with very little strain, would give the impression of a sudden liberation and modernization of the sensibility. Coupled with this is the attitude Mortmere cultivated, namely, the feeling that the problems of the world can be resolved by the word, and in particular, by the right word, the *mot juste*; in this sense, a phrase like "immeasureable neurotic dread" would seem to be possessed of a quasi-magical killing power. The sense that the word used imaginatively is somehow a very potent force in the political world is a holdover of a romantic idea of the imagination's power and, in particular, a modern form of Shelley's dictum; to a small group of intellectuals in England at this time, not yet disillusioned as to this fact by extensive political experience, not yet forced to define just what function literary speech did have in the political sphere, it must have seemed that they were entering upon a time when the imagination could have direct and practical bearing on politics.

A third reason that Auden was taken to be a generation's spokesman is the use of the public-school setting and his *enfant-terrible* tone. The appeal of these things does not mean merely that the generation had become conscious of the deficiencies of the traditional public-school system;

it means even more that, with what is called the "Auden generation," we see for the first time something similar to the modern cult of youth and revolution. For Auden's readers, a very limited group as Symons points out, the political conflict was one between members of the same class, divided into young and old; the young were reacting against what they felt to be the repressive system fostered by their parents and by people like their parents. They felt that they had themselves been affected by and deprived of something by this system; the best example of this is perhaps the criticism levelled against their schools and universities, that they had killed creative impulse and energy, fostered a homosexual fascist mentality, and intentionally kept their students emotionally immature, in order to guarantee their acquiescence to the system. Lawrence was often quoted by Auden's friends as condemning Oxford's "namby-pamby" undergraduate body, and one is led to believe that this comment struck them more forcibly than did most of his work.

Thus, within a small group at the beginning of the thirties, political interest was united with a youthful, optimistic, and naive desire to solve the problems of the public-school and university graduate; one sought to liberate stiffled creativity, to return to spontaneity, to free one's self from the Georgian atmosphere of the public school and to become modern in feeling and expression. For Auden, a unique figure in that he was thoroughly self-possessed and independent, personal liberation seems not to have been so important a motive; indeed, a large part of the appeal of Auden's early poetry would be its very freedom from the struggle of his contemporaries, its brash enthusiasm and ready absorption of the modern world.

From this sketchy discussion of Auden's poetry and the political atmosphere of the early thirties several additional points can be made that will have relevance for a consideration of Auden's later works. First, the idea of the enemy and the "Combine" preceded whatever form of Marxism that Auden later came to use and advocate; the Mortmere fantasies preceded, in fact, Auden's concern for society in any form, for they were developed when he was an undergraduate and still consciously apolitical. Second—something that must be remembered whenever one talks about any form of commitment in relation to Auden—part of Auden must be seen as indifferent to all matter of belief and, correspondingly, as indifferent to the content of his work. On the other side of all of Auden's professions of the moment lies a contentless, basic interest in the possibilities of expression in and of itself, in what can be done with the material rather than in the material itself, and in complications of style as self-sufficiently entertaining. In this way, Auden's work has affinities with such a phenomenon as the Camp mode of perception, with its combination of social awareness and political passivity. Like Camp, Auden's work represents a response to the world that is consciously self-indulgent and pleasure-oriented, that has a love of all that is stylistically complex for its own sake combined with a love of the extravagance of such complexity, which, in stylistic terms, combines a form of elegance with a cultivated awareness of the vulgar, and that makes a cult of the private amusement derived from these sources.

Isherwood's description of High Camp in *The World in the Evening* is, in this context, revealing:

"In any of your *voyages au bout de la nuit,* did you ever run across the word 'camp'?"

"I've heard people use it in bars. But I thought . . ."

"You thought it meant a swishy little boy with peroxided hair, dressed in a picture hat and a feather boa, pretending to be Marlene Dietrich? Yes, in queer circles, they call *that* camping. It's all very well in its place, but it's an utterly debased form. . . ." Charles' eyes shone delightedly. He seemed to be in the best of spirits, now, and thoroughly enjoying this exposition. "What *I* mean by camp is something much more fundamental. You can call the other Low Camp, if you like; then what I'm talking about is High Camp. High Camp is the whole emotional basis of the ballet, for example, and of course baroque art. You see, true High Camp always has an underlying seriousness. You can't camp about something you don't take seriously. You're not making fun of it; you're making fun out of it. You're expressing what's basically serious to you in terms of fun and artifice and elegance. Baroque art is largely camp about religion. The ballet is camp about love. . . . Do you see what I'm getting at?"

"I'm not sure. Give me some instances. What about Mozart?"

"Mozart's definitely a camp. Beethoven, on the other hand, isn't."

"Is Flaubert?"

"God, no!"

"And neither is Rembrandt?"

"No. Definitely not."

"But El Greco is?"

"Certainly."

"And so is Dostoevski?"

"Of course he is! In fact, he's the founder of the whole school of modern Psycho-Camp which was later developed by Freud."[31]

Much of Auden's work may not too unfairly be seen as of the spirit of High Camp; serious questions and emotions are developed in "terms of fun and artifice and elegance." Auden is well aware of the limitations of this way of absorbing ideas and relating to the artistic achievement of the past; as we shall see, he is at pains to indicate within his more mature work the way his poetic language reworks and even undercuts essentially serious issues and ideas that lie just outside the realm of the poem. Thus, the mythic world of the limestone landscape in "In Praise of Limestone" yields at points to a vision of a more serious surrounding world, one in which "the meaning of life" is "Something more than a mad camp." At the same time, however, Auden's deepest human and imaginative sympathies remain within that mythic world, for

> . . . when I try to imagine a faultless love
> Or the life to come, what I hear is the murmur
> Of underground streams, what I see is a limestone
> landscape.[32]

[31] New York: Random House, 1952, pp. 110–111.

[32] "In Praise of Limestone," *Nones* (New York: Random House, 1939), p. 16. Reprinted by permission of Faber and Faber, Ltd., and Random House, Inc.; copyright 1939, 1946, 1947, 1949, 1950, 1951, by W. H. Auden; copyright, 1950, by The Curtis Publishing Co.

3. Germany and England

To extend our consideration of Auden's relationship to a public world it is necessary to examine two different but overlapping encounters, his trip to the Germany of the Weimar Republic and subsequent experience in England of the thirties. These two encounters are closely related, not only biographically, but also in a less personal mannr; the political polarity of Weimar Germany could be and indeed was seen as a heightened dramatization of forces at work within England and Europe.

Auden's development into the leading political poet of the thirties began when he was still an undergraduate. As he wrote in 1965,

> By [G. E.] Moore standards, the Oxford of the twenties was frivolous indeed. At Cambridge in 1903, Pleasure was not, so Mr. Woolf tells us, considered a good; to us it was almost the only one. Looking back now, I find it incredible how secure life seemed. Too young for the war to have made any impression upon us, we imagined that the world was essentially the same as it had been in 1913, and we were far too insular and preoccupied with ourselves to know or

care what was going on across the channel. Revolution in Russia, inflation in Germany and Austria, Fascism in Italy, whatever fears or hopes they may have aroused in our elders, went unnoticed by us. Before 1930, I never opened a newspaper.[1]

The statement must, of course, be taken with a grain of salt, if only because Auden's retrospective comments on his early political beliefs are always to be mistrusted.

Nevertheless, the earlier Auden was hedonistic and frivolous, and these qualities were reflected in the social atmosphere of Oxford in the twenties; the high spirits and extravagant fantasy of his early political poetry reflect the persistence of this life style. Auden's first vaguely political act was carried out in such a spirit; during the general strike of 1926, he drove a car for the Trades Union Council with very little consciousness or concern for the political significance of the act.

It happened that a first cousin of mine, married to a stockbroker, lived a few doors away, so I paid a call. The three of us were just sitting down to lunch when her husband asked me if I had come up to London to be a Special Constable. "No, I said. "I am driving a car for the T.U.C." whereupon, to my utter astonishment, he ordered me to leave his house. It had never occurred to me that anybody took the General Strike seriously.[2]

One must observe Auden's political development as a

[1] "As It Seemed to Us," *The New Yorker*, 41 (April 3, 1965), 180.
[2] Ibid., p. 182.

growth away from—but never very far away from—such frivolity and detachment, and that growth occurred as radical politics, during the course of the thirties, consolidated itself and began to face crises of ever greater importance.

The experience crucial to Auden's later political development came at the end of his study at Oxford; though Auden's response to it may not have been immediate, it underlies almost all of his political writing in the thirties. When Auden left Oxford, his parents offered to finance a year abroad:

> The first personal choice I can remember making was my decision, when my father offered me a year abroad after I had gone down from Oxford, to spend it in Berlin. I knew no German and no German literature, but I felt out of sympathy with French culture, partly by temperament and partly in revolt against the generation of intellectuals immediately preceding mine, which was strongly Francophile. It is a decision [for which] I have been very thankful ever since.[3]

In Germany, Auden not only made great progress with the language—he recalled that he fell in love with the German language then—and made his first acquaintance with German literature, but also, more importantly, confronted a climate of thought and feeling upon which he would draw as he began to write political verse, at a time when England itself was developing a climate analogous to that of Germany. As one can observe by looking at the volume of Auden's poetry published by Spender in 1928,

---

[3] Ibid., p. 190.

it was only after his experience abroad that the political theme entered his work.

The year in Germany represented first and foremost a unique kind of mildly rebellious self-indulgence; it was, after all, not just a pilgrimage of a young writer to a center of continental culture but also a holiday trip to a modern Baby-lon, paid for by the young writer's parents. Berlin's sus-picious reputation in the eyes of the conventional English-man of the late twenties rested upon two bases. Germany had been the bitter enemy of England in World War I, and the rise, during the twenties, of sympathy for the Germans was not just a humanitarian response to the terrible economic condition of that land but also a slap in the face to the men of the Baldwin generation. More excit-ing, though, was the fact that Germany, in particular Berlin, came to represent to many young Englishmen a form of personal liberation, for, as Robert Graves and Alan Hodges somewhat spitefully put it, "in certain Berlin dancing-halls, it was pointed out, women danced only with women and men with men, Germany was the land of the free!"[4] With Auden, however, this liberation was more than simply sexual; in Berlin, he met John Layard and became enthusiastically involved in ideas derived primarily from the American psychologist Homer Lane, but which Auden would have been already prepared for by his wide reading in Freud and Freud's more whimsical forerunner, Georg Groddeck. These ideas, as Auden interpreted them, provided a partly comic, partly serious rationale for practical hedonism. Self-sacrifice was seen as the "subtlest

[4] *The Long Week-End* (New York: Norton, 1963), p. 101.

and most deadly form of selfishness," in that it implied "the sacrifice of others to yourself"; what was important was that one keep himself "pure-in-heart," and accomplishing this, no evil could prevail, not even sickness, for sickness was always the sign of a spiritual, not a physical disorder. One pragmatic deduction was of course clear: the pure-in-heart did not have to worry about venereal disease.

At the same time that it satisfied such ulterior motives, the Layard doctrine became one of Auden's early intellectual passions, and he adopted it in a way characteristically energetic and extravagant:

> Weston had assimilated all these ideas with his customary zest and ease, adding to them a touch of extravagance which was peculiarly his own. His whole vocabulary, I found, was renovated and revised to include the new catchwords. We hadn't been together a quarter of an hour before he was reproving me for harbouring a "death-wish." I had admitted to feeling ill:
>
> "You've got to drop all that," said Weston. "When people are ill, they're wicked. You must stop it. You must be pure in heart."
>
> "What nonsense!" I retorted. "How can I stop it? There's nothing the matter with my heart. It's my tonsils."
>
> "Your tonsils? That's very interesting. . . ." Weston's consulting-room manner was excessively irritating. "I suppose you know what *that* means?"
>
> "Certainly. It means I've caught a chill."
>
> "It means you've been telling lies!"
>
> "Oh, indeed? What have I been telling lies about?"

Weston looked down his nose, provokingly mysterious. I could have kicked him: "You're the only person who can answer that!"[5]

Just as he had formerly done at Oxford, Auden was using a partially comic and fantastic analysis to dominate his friends; not only had he "renovated" his vocabulary in terms of his new doctrine, but he had also thought out how his friends should be categorized in terms of it. As we have seen, Auden's attitude toward such a "belief" is difficult to pin down; although one notes his absoluteness of stricture when he tells Isherwood that he must "drop all that," one has the overwhelming impression that the conversation's seriousness is feigned, that Auden is playing the role of the bizarre physician and enjoying the chance to affect a "consulting-room manner."

Layard's effect on Auden's poetry is readily apparent; the extravagant fantasy of most of Auden's early work, from "Address for a Prize-Day" to "Consider this and in our time," owes a great deal to Layard's method of diagnosis, particularly to his belief that physical disorder has spiritual cause. Just why the contact with Layard should have had such a decisive effect on Auden is more difficult to ascertain; the answer seems to lie in a combination of factors. Superficially, Layard's doctrine provided a very handy rationale for practical hedonism; on a deeper level, it gave Auden a relatively literal rendering of ideas about the self that had intrigued him in his previous reading of D. H. Lawrence. More important was the fact that the

[5] Christopher Isherwood, *Lions and Shadows* (Norfolk: New Directions, 1947), pp. 301–303.

Layard doctrine struck exactly the right tone; it was a blend of the bizarre and the serious that would have been very congenial to a Mortmere fantasist, and quite probably it was incorporated into the Mortmere landscape by Auden and Isherwood together in Berlin, even before the composition of such poems as "Consider this and in our time."

Most important, though, was that this peculiar tone was simultaneously realized in the Berlin cultural milieu: private eccentricity became united, in a marvelously fruitful way, with public reality. In Berlin, Auden lived in a world simultaneously bohemian, fantastic, and yet, in a sense, comfortable; as he wrote in "Letter to Lord Byron," he "lived with crooks but seldom was molested."[6] The social and cultural atmosphere was one in which a Mortmerian fantasist would not only be particularly interested, but also would feel quite at home; in Berlin, reality might well seem capable of equaling anything that the most extravagant fantasy could ever produce for itself. As Istvan Deak notes in *Weimar Germany's Left-Wing Intellectuals,*

> Berlin harbored those who elsewhere might have been subjected to ridicule or persecution. Comintern agents, Dadaist poets, expressionist painters, anarchist philosophers, *Sexualwissenschaftler,* vegetarian and Esperantist prophets of a new humanity, *Schnorrer* ("freeloaders"—artists of coffeehouse indolence), courtesans, homosexuals, drug addicts, naked dancers, and apostles of nudist self-liberation, black marketeers, embezzlers,

[6] Auden and Louis MacNeice, *Letters from Iceland* (New York: Random House, 1937), p. 210. Selections from *Letters to Iceland* reprinted by permission of Random House, copyright, 1939, by **W. H. Auden.**

and professional criminals flourished in a city which was hungry for the new, the sensational and the extreme. Moreover, Berlin became the cultural center of Central and Eastern Europe as well.[7]

In becoming a disciple of Layard, Auden was not only indulging his own spirit of extravagance, but also participating in Berlin's peculiar blend of novelty, eccentricity, disreputable ferment, caricature evil, and Dadaist innocence; to put it most graphically, in Berlin, George Grosz seemed to some observers not to be a caricaturist but a reporter.[8] Germany had, by the time of Auden's arrival, entered into a period of relative financial stability reflected in a slackening of its cultural energy; nevertheless, there was still much in Berlin's cabaret and theater to testify to the continuance of the peculiar vividness of the early twenties.

To define just what in this atmosphere was most important to Auden's development, it is necessary to isolate three topics: the cultivation and deepening of an eccentric fantasy, the avant-garde propensity for making aesthetic use of popular culture, and the attempt to relate art to politics. The first topic corresponds to one of Auden's deepest imaginative impulses; this impulse did not manifest itself in his art in any meaningful way until after his time in Berlin. One trait that distinguishes the poems written after Berlin most noticeably from those written before is the extensive and wholehearted use of parody and caricature; it is only after Berlin, for example, that Auden wrote the energetic, high-level caricature of such poems as "Consider

[7] Berkeley: University of California Press, 1968, pp. 14–15.
[8] Peter Gay, *Weimar Culture: The Outsider as Insider* (New York: Harper and Row, 1968), p. 70.

this and in our time." This development found its most notable literary analogues in the cabaret and in theatrical performances like Piscator's 1928 version of *Schwejk*, for which Grosz did an animated film; it can, as we have seen, also be more generally related to the tone of the times in Berlin.

Auden's most vivid and uninhibited use in poetry of elements of popular culture began with the schoolboy setting for *Paid*, which was, although first suggested by Isherwood in England, not written until Auden's stay in Berlin; more significant were the creation of figures like the Airman and the introduction into *Poems* (1930) of types like the "insufficient units" congregated in the Sport Hotel or the anarchist with his "arm-pit secrecy," types that one would find in detective or spy stories.[9] To be sure, "The Secret Agent" was already written by this time, and much of the Mortmere lore had been put into settings drawn from popular thrillers; nevertheless, there was a significant development in Auden's use of popular culture between *Poems* (1928), which is often serious in tone and for the most part derivative from exclusively literary sources, in particular Eliot, Hardy, and Lawrence, and the *Poems* (1930), in which Auden's fantasy expands to make use of a great variety of material from popular culture and social reality. The Berlin milieu did not so much alter Auden in this respect as it brought out already existant aspects of his poetic character.

The most dramatic development in Auden's work after his time in Berlin lies in the realm of subject matter for

[9] Poem XXIX and Poem I of *Poems* (London: Faber and Faber, 1930).

poetry; it was only with the publication of *Poems* (1930) that Auden became an explicitly political poet. That Berlin was, in a general sense, a crucial factor in this development is obvious; the connection between art and politics in Germany during the Weimar years was so close that there was scarcely an artistic document that could not be seen within a political context. One can argue with Peter Gay that Germany was then the "only country that could have taken seriously Shelley's famous sweeping dictum that 'poets are the unacknowledged legislators of the world.' "[10] To give a full summary of the relationships between art and politics in Weimar would be impossible here; it would involve writing a complete cultural history of the Weimar Republic. But the extent and range of these connections can be suggested: the decade of the twenties was a great era for the political cabaret; films were obsessively concerned with political themes, considerations of the nature of tyranny, freedom, and man's fate in modern society; Expressionism was an artistic and literary movement of explicit and sometimes violent political significance, and some Expressionist artists attempted to act in political roles; there were a number of literary-political journals which exerted sometimes a genuine political leverage; and poets like Rainer Maria Rilke and Stefan George, who were not politically tendentious in their work, were given politically significant interpretations.[11] Even in the conception of the Weimar

[10] Gay, p. 67.

[11] George had considerable political effect through the group mystique of the George-Kreis. For a lengthy discussion of these topics, see: on the cabaret, Heinz Greul, *Bretter, die die Zeit bedeuten* (Cologne: Kiepenhauer and Witsch, 1961); on the film,

Republic itself, literature and politics were linked: the Weimar government was to be a fulfillment of the German humanist tradition, and it looked to Goethe and Schiller for its models.

There are several ways to examine the effect of this atmosphere of interrelated political and artistic ferment on Auden's work; did Auden assimilate into his poetry any fundamentally German political themes and did he come under any particular literary influence in his handling of political matter? The first question is perhaps the easier to answer; there is a remarkable correspondence between the themes of Auden's early poetry and certain aspects of Weimar politics and culture. In Berlin, Auden encountered, in a new and dramatic form, many of the preoccupations, worries, and interests of his generation in England; as is always the case with Auden, whether traveling to Berlin or Iceland, or reading Freud, Marx, or Kierkegaard, one senses that he has gone there only to meet something of himself. The idea of a death instinct at work in the ill, repressed self, an idea he picked up in explicit form from Layard, was, on the one hand, to be found in his and his friends' early interest in D. H. Lawrence; on the other hand, as Gay makes clear in his book, the action of a death wish on the societal level was more than evident in German culture, something which Auden was himself quick to apply to England in the political verse he wrote after Berlin. Similarly,

Siegfried Kracauer, *From Caligari to Hitler* (Princeton, N.J.: Princeton University Press, 1947); on the tangled political significance of the Expressionist movement, Walter Sokel, *The Writer in Extremis* (Stanford, Cal.: Stanford University Press, 1959); on the best of the political-literary journals, *Die Weltbühne*, Deak; and on the cultural influence of the poets, Gay.

two chief themes of Auden's early work, the cult of youth and the youthful hero, are to be found both in England, in the reaction of the Auden generation against the public-school system, and in a Germany preoccupied with the politically critical conflict of the son and the father, be this conflict dramatized in literature or in such phenomena as the *Wandervogel* movements.[12] What happened, then, was that Auden had a stroke of exceptionally good fortune. As a developing poet, equipped with an immense knowledge of and infatuation with psychology, but with no political experience, he encountered a culture to which psychological analysis had a singular political relevance and in which he could thus see, acted out far more dramatically than in England, conflicts that would be the major issues of his time. Auden's grasp at first of the political implications of many of his ideas was shaky, as is well illustrated by his nearly uncritical enthusiasm for the ideas of D. H. Lawrence and for hero figures like T. E. Lawrence; nevertheless, having the example of Germany always before him throughout the thirties, he was able to develop the most effective antifascist poetic polemic of the decade.

The question of whether there were any specifically literary influences on Auden's handling of political themes is more difficult to answer; it is best to limit our focus to the one literary source scholars have singled out as being crucial to Auden's development, the work of Bertolt Brecht. The prevailing view, that Auden was heavily influenced by Brecht's epic theater, has recently come under some sensible attack by Breon Mitchell:

[12] See Gay, Chapters 3, 5, and 6.

As for Brecht, Auden was certainly influenced to some degree by the *Dreigroschenoper* and *Mahagonny*, the first of which he saw while in Berlin (1928), but, we must remember, at a time when he was only beginning to learn German. He was also familiar with some of the songs from *Mahagonny* which had been printed at this time in the *Hauspostille* collection. The play itself was not produced in Berlin until 21 December, 1931. Auden feels the influence upon his plays to have been slight at best, and certainly not of major importance. (This is not to deny a more profound influence upon his poetry. He had read and enjoyed Brecht's *Hauspostille* poems (1927), as mentioned above, but feels this did not influence his plays. He still prefers Brecht's lyric poetry to the dramatic works.) Thus he says that an attempt to pin down a major influence to Brecht in the 1930's would be 'very wrong.'[13]

The argument is perhaps too strongly presented. Auden's progress with German was described by Isherwood as astoundingly rapid, and it does not in any event take a very great command of a language to appreciate a theatrical production; Auden's own comments may be interpreted in part as the understandable irritation of an author whose dramatic work has been repeatedly judged as imitative. There is, however, much truth to the general point that the attempt to trace a specific and definitive influence to Brecht is one that makes too much out of a relatively limited literary contact; Mitchell's discovery of other sources

[13] Breon Mitchell, "W. H. Auden and Christopher Isherwood: The 'German Influence,'" *Oxford German Studies*, 1 (1966), 165.

for Auden's plays, most importantly Cocteau, Ibsen, and the English Christmas pantomime, and his observation that, in Berlin, Auden was perhaps more interested in the film and the cabaret than he was in the theater, are strong supporting arguments.

There remains despite Mitchell's persuasiveness, the firm sense that Auden is the English equivalent of the Brecht who wrote *Die Dreigroschenoper* (*Threepenny Opera*) and *Mahagonny;* it is this sense, as much as any concrete biographical information, that has prompted scholars to link the two writers. As soon as one ceases to try to prove Brecht's direct influence on Auden, an attempt that generally limits itself to a discussion of the theater, the similarities between them become all the more interesting; they both sought solutions to the problem of political *engagement* through literature, something which concerns general artistic strategy and which is not confined to work within any particular genre. That Brecht and Auden should be strikingly similar in their handling of political material would not be odd, even if Auden had never seen a play or read a poem by Brecht: both were attempting to find an artistic voice for a left-wing polemic; both were concerned with avant-garde innovation in art; and both were interested in techniques of satire which were then being used in the political cabaret.

One of the best representations of Brecht's thought at this time (1927–1931) and of those ideas that are most pertinent to a description of Auden's development is found in his opera-dramas *Aufstieg und Fall der Stadt Mahagonny* and *Die Dreigroschenoper*, for which he wrote critical notes. With *Mahagonny*, Brecht described himself as attempting to subvert traditional opera from within:

The opera *Mahagonny* pays conscious tribute to the senselessness of the operatic form. The irrationality of the opera lies in the fact that rational elements are employed, solid reality is aimed at, but at the same time it is all washed out by the music. A dying man is real. If at the same time he sings we are translated to the sphere of the irrational. . . . The more unreal and unclear the music can make the reality . . . the more pleasurable the whole process becomes: the pleasure grows in proportion to the degree of unreality.[14]

One could imagine the relevance of such a description to the music of Wagner; with Brecht, however, "the intention was that a certain unreality, irrationality and lack of seriousness should be introduced at the right moment, and so strike with a double meaning."[15] The irrationality and unreality of which Brecht speaks, then, is not that of a "love affair with death,"[16] Peter Gay's phrase for the prevailing literary-political atmosphere of Weimar Germany; it is just the opposite, for it is equated with a lack of seriousness, and it leads, by means of its very indulgence in fun, to a critique of pleasure rather than a yielding to it, an immersion in the aesthetic experience. Brecht is explicit on this point: "As for the content of this opera, *its content is pleasure*. Fun, in other words, not only as form but as subject-matter."[17] In such a poem as "Consider this and in our time," Auden is attempting to reach the same goal; his por-

---

[14] *Brecht on Theatre*, trans. John Willett (New York: Hill and Wang, 1966), pp. 35–36.

[15] Ibid., p. 36.

[16] Gay, p. 62.

[17] Brecht, p. 36.

trayal of the death of civilization is at the same time pleasurable and a critique of pleasure, and the poem's intentionally operatic rhetoric—its unreality, its seeming lack of
seriousness, and its generally high spirits—serves to under-
score this critique.

What lies most clearly behind such a critique of pleasure
is a new evaluation of the aesthetic experience. Inflated
rhetoric, improbability, and lack of seriousness are all used
to prevent too great an absorption in the aesthetic experience; thus, in Brecht's formulation of the epic theater, "the
spectator adopts an attitude of smoking-and-watching. Such
an attitude on his part at once compels a better and clearer
performance as it is hopeless to try to 'carry away' any
man who is smoking and accordingly pretty well occupied
with himself."[18] Brecht sought to induce this attitude by a
number of means, all of which aimed at preventing too
great an emotional involvement in the opera and at giving
the drama didactic energy; the most famous critical term
for these techniques is the *Verfremdungseffekt* (alienation
effect). To define just what Brecht meant by this term is
perhaps as difficult a venture as hunting a Snark: his use of
the term is too varied and the difficulty of actually applying it to his dramas is too immense. But some points seem
clear enough to state modestly; the effect depends on establishing critical distance from the surface of the drama
by a variety of devices. The action of the play can be
broken off, so that the sustained emotion necessary for simple involvement is rendered impossible; suspense can be
eliminated by means of signs that summarize the action of

[18] Ibid., p. 44.

each scene before it is played; the turning points of the play can be underscored as such, so that one becomes critically aware of their theatricality; and the actors can be overtrained so that they do not involve themselves in their parts, but rather indicate them.

The similarity of such ideas to Auden's work is striking. First and foremost, through them comes a theoretical basis for the spirit of fun; high spirits could be put, as in *Mahagonny*, at the service of a moral and even political point. More particularly, the techniques of Brecht's epic theater and *Verfremdungseffekt* correlate with a number of Auden's specific rhetorical practices: Auden's own propensity to quick changes in and explosions of poetic mood, his use of a wide range of rhetoric and diction that calls attention to itself as such, and his cultivation of a poetic structure that is intentionally nonorganic would be the most important examples. Finally, one can see a closeness to Brecht's aesthetics in Auden's lifelong preoccupation with and criticism of the role of art, both in society and in human psychology; like Brecht, Auden was a confirmed opponent of uncritical immersion in aesthetic experience, seeing the political, psychological, and spiritual dangers of such a release from critical and rational consciousness, and this tendency runs throughout all his different periods, from the poems of the early thirties to his Marxist plays, to *The Sea and the Mirror*, and to later poems like "Pleasure Island."

There are, at the same time, several important distinctions between Auden and Brecht in terms of their politically oriented aesthetics. For Auden, these ideas were not so revolutionary in tendency as they were for Brecht, a fact that has its roots both in differences of personality and of literary tradition. The idea of cultivating "fun" in art was for Brecht a direct blow at the prevailing German reverence for art and the artist; in England "fun" was not nearly so tendentious a literary mode. Thus, with Auden, such Brechtian techniques as the use of diction that calls attention to itself as such would represent as much a personality trait as part of a rhetoric consciously formed with regard to its aesthetic-political point; Auden's display of style has always been a part of his poetry, and, as is evident in his use of clashing vocabulary in his later poems, it represents at heart an elegantly comic love of verbal play which gives one a new and more conscious perspective on the thing so depicted and which may be then put in the service of a number of different ideas, ranging from revolutionary politics to his later self-appointed task of defending "civilization" against the inroads of leveling barbarians. Parallel to this distinction is the fact that political and aesthetic revolution was something of different emotional importance for the two authors. With Brecht, creativity and revolutionary polemic were much more deeply entwined than with Auden, for whom revolutionary tendentiousness remains more a form of individualistic extravagance than inner necessity. Auden never worried, as Brecht did, about the gap between his theoretical pronouncements on the function of art and his own practice, nor did he ever undertake major changes in poetic style on political grounds, nor did he ever involve himself so deeply as Brecht in directly propagandistic didacticism.

There is one further way in which Brecht's work is strikingly similar to that of Auden: both were concerned with absorbing elements of popular culture into art. Not only did Brecht try to turn a great many popular genres into literary or quasi-literary ones—as the popular song and musical revue—but he also drew upon popular culture for much of the substance of certain of his dramas. For example, *Mann ist Mann* is a half-romantic, half-satirical play upon a Kiplingesque world[19] and *Mahagonny* is an epitome of the German conception of the wealth, decadence, and violence of America; similarly, the world of sports yields metaphors, ideas, and settings for Brecht's writings in all genres. Brecht saw his use of such material in the context of his larger battle against literary tradition and the political establishment:

> Our dramatic form is based on the spectator's ability to be carried along, identify himself, feel empathy and understand. To put it bluntly, for those in the business: a play that is set, say, in a wheat exchange isn't suited to major, dramatic form. While it's hard for us to imagine a time and adopt an attitude in which such a situation does not seem natural, our *successors* will observe such an unnatural and incomprehensible situation with amazement. So what ought our major form to be like?
>
> Epic. It must report. It must not believe that one can identify oneself with our world by empathy, nor must it want this. The subject-matter is immense; our choice of dramatic means must take account of the fact.[20]

[19] John Willett, *The Theatre of Bertolt Brecht* (New York: New Directions, 1968), p. 72.

[20] Brecht, p. 25.

The use of such artistic settings, ones that are drawn from a modern, unpoetic sphere, is an avant-garde attempt to update art, to make it modern:

> The new school of play-writing must systematically see to it that its form includes 'experiment.' It must be free to use connections on every side; it needs equilibrium and has a tension which governs its component parts and 'loads' them against one another. (Thus this form is anything but a revue-like sequence of sketches.)[21]

More than this, it represents an artistic practice with political tendency, especially for Germany, where the aspiration for wholeness and cultural unity implicit in the work of poets of *Kultur* "turns out on examination to be a great regression born from a great fear: the fear of modernity."[22]

Auden in the thirties was also a poet of experiment, of conscious cultivation of novelty in form and material, and was so in much the same sense; in the "charade," *Paid on Both Sides*, in *The Orators*, *The Dance of Death*, the plays for the Group Theater, and the literary travel book, *Letters from Iceland*, Auden attempted an experiment with both the mixing of different genres and the juxtaposition of differing kinds of content, and one of the principal reasons for the sense of freedom, of poetic liberation, that his work gave his contemporaries was just this use of "connections on every side." One of the principal faults of Auden's dramatic works is that from which Brecht was trying to distinguish his epic theater, namely the degeneration of ex-

[21] Ibid., p. 46.
[22] Gay, p. 96.

periment, overenthusiastic about its own novelty, into a "revue-like" series of sketches. For Auden, even more than for Brecht, this would have been the most likely pitfall of such an artistic technique; since Auden was more playful in his experimentation than was Brecht, he was much more likely to use his material in an incidental and sketch-like manner.

Our speculations about Berlin and all that Auden encountered there have been surprisingly extensive in the light of the little that is known about his trip; what they represent is the attempt to pry into and explain an experience that had a decided effect on his writing and that Auden himself has repeatedly described as a major event in his life. When Breon Mitchell cites Auden as saying about his German experience that "I was awakened in that for the first time I felt the shaking of the foundations of things,"[23] we may note with amusement, perhaps, the voice of the Existential Christian who has read his Tillich; at the same time, it is interesting to contrast this remark with our description above of Auden's stay in Berlin. What shook the foundations was an encounter with "loony Layard,"[24] with a land of homosexual freedom, and with a city of artistic ferment and political upheaval which gave a dramatic external justification to much that was latent in Auden's sensibility; it is an odd mixture of extravagance, enjoyment, and, nevertheless, educative encounter. But just such a mixture is what seems most impressive and amusing about Au-

[23] Mitchell, p. 166.
[24] Auden, *The Orators* (London: Faber and Faber, 1932), Ode I. In the later edition, the line was altered to "the suave archdeacon."

den at the beginning of his poetic career; a political situation of unrelieved and humorless oppression would only
have served either to drive Auden away or to quell a poetic
energy that had been hitherto "extraordinary and false."[25]
Instead, an atmosphere that was not only receptive to such
energies but also indicated ways of directing them against
genuine targets was what Auden needed in order to grow
creatively; this was just what he found in Berlin.

Just how concretely Auden's experience in Germany
manifests itself in his work can be seen from *The Dance of
Death;* written at the time of Hitler's assumption of power
(an event that came to the English radicals as "the greatest
single shock" of the decade),[26] it is a conscious attempt to
come to grips with the matter of Germany and to find a
way of integrating it into the English political scene. The
principal theme of *Dance,* the way a "death wish" operates
on a societal level, is one acquired in Germany; since then,
its relevance to the English political situation had become
popularized by John Strachey's immensely influential book
The Coming Struggle for Power. The setting of the drama
is in large part also one derived from Germany and trans-
planted into England. The English fad of the health club
was one taken over from Germany and the ideal it es-
pouses, that of fostering a purely physical health by refus-
ing the "invitation / To self-examination,"[27] corresponds
to Spender's description of the effect of the Weimar Republic upon himself and his friends: "there was something

[25] Auden, *Look, Stranger!* (London: Faber and Faber, 1936), p. 64.

[26] Symons, *The Thirties* (London, Cresset Press, 1960), p. 40.

[27] *The Dance of Death* (London: Faber and Faber, 1933), p. 8.

exclusive about this Germany which included the bronzed, the athletic, the good-looking and the smart, but shut out the old, the intellectual and the ugly."[28] More important, this cult of youth and the athletic could mask, as it did in the *Wandervogel* movement, an essentially fascist mentality. This movement, according to Istvan Deak, begun "in symbolic protest against the grimness of city life and the banalities of bourgeois society[,] . . . found support for its ideals in the elitist doctrine of the poet Stefan George who saw the irrational (poetic) essence of man as the regenerative force within politics and society."[29] Although the movement was a forerunner to both the Hitler *Jugend* and the communist *Freie Jugend*, its political tendency was, in the Weimar years, principally nationalist and virulently anti-Semitic. Most explicit is the superimposing of Germany onto England that is accomplished in the course of the drama; by doing so, Auden hopes to portray the fact that the capitalist crisis, as seen by Marx, is not a local but an international phenomenon. In the middle of the play, just as the chorus begins to threaten revolution against the Dancer and the society he represents, the Announcer steps forward to make a sinister and intentionally confusing announcement:

> *Announcer:* Comrades, I absolutely agree with you. We must have a revolution. But wait a moment. All this talk about class war won't get us anywhere. The circumstances here are quite different from Russia.

[28] Stephen Spender, *World within World* (London: Hamish Hamilton, 1951), p. 108.

[29] Deak, p. 287.

Russia has no middle class, no tradition of official administrative service. We must have an English revolution suited to English conditions, a revolution not to put one class on top but to abolish class, to ensure not less for some but more for all, a revolution of Englishmen for Englishmen. After all, are we not all of one blood, the blood of King Arthur, and Wayland the Smith? We have Lancelot's courage, Merlin's wisdom. Our first duty is to keep the race pure, and not let these dirty foreigners come in and take our job. Down with the dictatorship of international capital. Away with their filthy books which corrupt our innocent sons and daughters. English justice, English morals, England for the English.[30]

The announcer manages to win over the chorus by first garbling Marx and then allowing just about all the insidious doctrines of fascism to creep up to the surface; he brings them over to a pure German fascism in English clothing, emphasizing such ideals as *Blut und Boden*, the primitive and heroic myths of England, and the purity of the race, and then advocating action that is the logical consequence of these ideals, racist persecution and book-burning.

To engage in an extended analysis of *The Dance of Death* is not necessary here; it is far from a successful play and ranks among the least interesting of Auden's works. One need only add that, after a great deal of incidental, high-spirited parody, the Dancer does die and the old society is overthrown; the moment is announced by the play's *deus ex machina*, Mr. Karl Marx: "The instruments of pro-

[30] Page 17.

duction have been too much for him. He is liquidated."[31]
This conclusion raises as many problems as it solves, and it
will be helpful to our discussion of English and German
politics to try to deal with them. Marx's appearance marks
the fulfillment of the play's thematic intent, the dramatization of the fall of capitalism; his entrance, however, is patently absurd, especially since he is greeted with an updated
version of the wedding march.

The blend of parody, the absurd, and sheer fun with a
political theme is quite familiar to us by now, for, in essence, the play's tone, its particular tendentiousness, paral-
lels that of "Consider this," the major differences between
them being the lack of linguistic sophistication of the play
and its lesser concern with psychological analysis, differences necessitated in part by its genre, the fast-paced revue.
In a broader sense, the play can be seen as similar to *Mahagonny*, about which Brecht made the comment:

> Perhaps *Mahagonny* is as culinary as ever—just as culi-
> nary as an opera ought to be—but one of its functions
> is to change society; it brings the culinary principle
> under discussion, it attacks the society that needs op-
> eras of such a sort; it still perches happily on the old
> bough, perhaps, but at least it has started . . . to saw
> it through. . . . And here you have the effect of the
> innovations and the song they sing. Real innovations
> attack the roots.[32]

The Dance of Death, as is pointed up by the unsavory way
in which Sir Edward keeps the play going, shares with

[31] Ibid., p. 38.
[32] Brecht, p. 41.

Mahagonny the difficult status of a piece written for entertainment which is at the same time attacking the very idea of entertainment and the society that fosters it. With Auden, however, the relationship of entertainment to a moral tone is exceedingly problematic; the dilemma becomes most clear with regard to the appearance of Marx. The backbone of the play is a kind of Marxist analysis, yet Marx at the end makes, to the tune of the wedding march, a most absurd entrance.

The reasons for this ambiguity are several. Most clearly, Auden's sensibility is much lighter and more high-spirited than Brecht's; whereas behind *Mahagonny*'s "fun" is something extremely grotesque, a sense of deadly sins, one feels that in Auden the surface action is the important thing and that the play depends on Auden's coming up again and again with some new engaging effect and scene. Such a sense of fun is exceedingly difficult to turn off, especially at those times when one "should" turn it off; thus the stream of exaggerated incidents sweeps on into the biggest comic exaggeration of all, the appearance of Marx at the end.

In the context of Auden's relationship to left-wing politics of the time, however, a more interesting explanation can be found. The English radical movement of the thirties was still in its infancy and, although Hitler had just come to power in Germany, the historical situation was not yet one of extreme crisis, as it was later in the decade; intellectuals in both England and Germany, although terribly disillusioned by the collapse of the Weimar Republic, felt at first that Hitler was not so much a serious threat as he was a bad joke. Moreover, the perception of fascism as a threatening force inside English society would always have to remain something a little extravagant in tone, for, in England, the fascist movement struck too many essentially alien notes ever to blossom, a feeling implicit in the absurd comedy of the Announcer's demogogic oration in which German fascism is put point by point into English dress. Thus the British Union of Fascists (B.U.F.) was never to become a power, for, as Michael Wharton writes in his essay "A Few Lost Causes,"

> Mosley had carefully studied the methods of Fascist movements abroad and copied them, too slavishly for his ultimate advantage. The Blackshirt uniform, the theatrical floodlit meetings with stylized salutes and cries of "Hail Mosley!", the para-military organization—all these were profoundly and perhaps fatally un-English.[33]

As a result, Strachey's vision of England progressing toward a crisis in which either a fascist or a communist government would emerge in control was more an abstract and intellectual drama than it was an immediate threat, and the transference of what was in Germany a more earnest polarity—that between the left wing and a fascist right integrated with the vested economic and cultural interests—onto the less seriously polarized English political scene would give that polarity something of an imported and willful character. The caricatures arising therefrom would thus tend more toward exaggerated fictions and comic abuse than they would toward bitter political grotesques.

[33] *The Baldwin Age* (London: Eyre and Spottiswoode, 1960), p. 88.

Auden's encounter with Weimar Germany provided him not only with much of the matter and manner of his poetry, but also with the occasion for rapid intellectual and poetic growth; the chief reason for this sudden growth is that, in Germany, he discovered a public world that mirrored and thus realized many of the traits of his private sensibility. Auden's experience in the England of the thirties is of a similar nature; he associated with a group of artists and intellectuals, who, through the climate of belief and action they created, helped him to give his distinctive talents a public focus and to realize many of his ideas and attitudes in a more accessible way than hitherto possible.

The English radical intellectuals in the thirties took part in a variety of activities, ranging from a revolution in poetry, the bringing together of a new literary-political audience in the Left Book Club, an intense interest in communism and specifically in Russia, to concrete political issues like the Spanish Civil War, the struggle against fascism in general, and protests over the economic crises. But for all the seeming clarity of the issues and the obvious polarization of the left against center and right, this movement remains exceedingly complex; it was built upon a fabric of interesting contradictions and tensions, without which it could never have taken so firm a hold upon the intellectuals' imaginations, consciences, and hearts. It is most important for an understanding of Auden's development to try to analyze the movement in terms of these contradictions.

Two views of the intellectual radicals of the thirties must be dealt with at the very start. Their movement was neither simply one of moral outrage nor one of desperate, alienated

young men reacting against the wasteland of early twentieth-century society, a society which had lost its belief in
itself; the tone of the movement is far more complex than
these attitudes suggest. Both moral fervor and personal des-
peration are qualified in a number of important ways. The
intellectual radicals of the thirties were seldom persecuted
for their beliefs or their activities and were not often ostra-
cized socially; on the contrary, they attracted considerable
and often very flattering attention, so that, a small minor-
ity, they seem to us even now to *be* the thirties. Moreover,
the political groups formed then were simultaneously social
ones; their formation, even when intellectual and proletar-
ian were brought together, did not represent the emergence
of a volatile, bohemian culture (better, anticulture), but
rather a shift in social groupings, the creation of a new social environment either more vigorous and meaningful than
the normal one, in that friendships would be based on a
sense of common purpose as well as upon ordinary socia-
bility, or simply more boring than the normal one, in that
people who had no personal interests in common found
themselves forced together. The role of the "fellow traveler" is a further indication of the relaxed atmosphere
of thirties' politics; to be a "fellow traveler" can be to revolt in comfort, a comfort suggested by Philip Toynbee's
comment that "the politics of middle-class intellectuals in
those days were really a kind of hobby—a passionate stimu-
lant rather than a burdensome and cruel necessity."[34]

The intellectual radicals were, according to Neal Wood's
exposition in *Communism and British Intellectuals,*

[34] As quoted in Francis Hope, "Then and Now," *The Review,*
11–12 (1964), 3.

concentrated almost entirely in London, Oxford and Cambridge—where the children of the leisure classes were educated. The majority of the left-wing activities were to be found among the students of the arts and certain of the sciences, particularly biology and physics. Very few of those studying for the professions of law, medicine, and engineering seemed to be inclined in this direction.[35]

They were thus, from the start, in an odd and contrary position. On the one hand, they were in revolt against the system whose most hopeful sons they were, and, accordingly, they were to be found in the nonproductive and theoretical areas of study. The marginal status of these disciplines was accentuated by the economic conditions of the time; when they

went down from their universities for the last time, they faced the problem of employment in a society in which jobs for young bourgeois graduates were at a premium. Many of the scientists stayed on to pursue research in their universities. A few of the arts graduates like Hill and Thomson found their niche in the academic world. A great many of the poets and writers, in the absence of a ready patronage, became journalists. Others turned to teaching, tutoring, and giving English lessons at home and abroad.[36]

On the other hand, they retained in a number of ways their status as children of the middle class. Most important, they

[35] New York: Columbia University Press, 1959, p. 53.
[36] Ibid., p. 88.

were seen as a group and, despite all bridging of social bar-
riers, they remained in essence first a group of young graduates from the best schools and second members of the
burgeoning English "radical family," a family which for
many had the added charm of having a firm sense of being
"in." Also, their group was itself something that could be
seen as far from alien to English traditions; Neal Wood
quotes John Maynard Keynes on this point:

> There is no one in politics today worth sixpence out-
> side the ranks of liberals except the post-war gen-
> eration of intellectual communists under thirty-five.
> Them, too, I like and respect. Perhaps in their feelings
> and instincts they are the nearest thing we have to the
> typical nervous nonconformist English gentleman who
> went to the Crusades, made the Reformation, fought
> the Great Rebellion, won our civil and religious liber-
> ties and humanized the working classes last century.[37]

This comment is in fact not so far from the truth as it
may seem; not only is it true in terms of the backgrounds
of the left-wing intellectuals, but also it suggests a way in
which their politics may be interpreted. Much of the communism of the thirties can be explained as the attempt to
find a position from which a kind of independent criticism
can be leveled at society. The rise of the view of society
as a "system" places new burdens upon those who wish to
exercise the traditional right to free discourse; since, to
those who hold this view, all who operate within the system are, by definition, either corrupted or absorbed by it

[37] Ibid., p. 41.

and since the system is so stable as to remain ultimately un-affected by mere voiced criticism, there is a great pressure on one to assert his individuality by joining or publicly sympathizing with an extraparliamentary party, something both convenient and possible in the thirties, as to do so did not necessarily make great demands on one's private free-dom or even time.

But to rest with this explanation would be to ignore all that was genuinely revolutionary about the thirties. Indeed, its vital center is located in problems of a deeper and often personal nature, problems that were interrelated with the political conflict. The most important of these were the re-volt of the young against a society controlled by their par-ents or people like their parents and, in conjunction with this revolt, the attempt to find a new form of self-expres-sion and self-realization in the face of "established" reality. The impulse to revolt and self-realization took, in England, a variety of forms, ranging from the outbreak, as in Au-den's early work, of an extravagant nonsense, to a satirical reexamination of the old by a new rationalist consciousness derived from the thought of Freud and Marx, to a vigorous revolt against the sexual mores of the established society, to unrest in and criticism of the educational system, to an ex-plicitly political activism on the part of a group who, un-like the communist intellectuals of the twenties, came to left-wing politics with little or no prior experience.

The explicitly political side of the intellectuals' radical-ism began in a great deal of uncertainty as to its own na-ture; the principal impulse behind it was, at first, not politi-cally defined and by its nature only partly susceptible of political definition. What people called for was "action" per se, as an alternative to what was seen as a stagnant government and political structure; implicit here is the consternation of the young at finding themselves in a society geared to stability and the status quo, as both Baldwin's government and Baldwin's personality seemed to be, and this consternation expressed itself in a number of ways. It was revealed most simply in a horror of the dull and an irrepressible urge to parody everything that was part of the given and staid order, or, more deeply, in an antipathy to all that seemed repressive of personal impulse, indistinguishable from creative energy when seen from this standpoint, or, more intensely, in a form of moral agony closely related to the sense of stifled self-expression, a moral sensitivity that reacts almost selectively to those evils that maintain themselves under what seems to be the leaden and hypocritical guise of an established order, under a blind, middle-class moral smugness and safety, and under the rhetoric of the reasonable compromise and the necessary slowness of all change.

The early confusion of such an activism can be seen in several ways. In politics, it is interesting to note how the career of John Strachey as an extraparliamentary politician began first in association with Oswald Mosley, the founder of the British Union of Fascists; the primary impulse was for him to set up a party of "action" outside the existing system. Among the literary intellectuals one notes the early attempt to mix D. H. Lawrence's interest in the unconscious and in the achievement of a transcendental and passionate wholeness with the rationalism of Marx and Freud, who were themselves, in many ways, quite incompatible; this mixture of thought was symptomatic of a mixture of motive as well, for at the same time the literary intellectual was attempting to bring about the "just society" he was attempting to achieve for himself a new kind of liberation, importance, and power. One example of this lies in the very attempt to blend art with politics; a new kind of power would accrue to art if one could find a way of applying it to the class struggle that would not mean reducing it to the level of mere propaganda, for, through a union with a just and historically justified cause, art would become something more than mere decoration and aesthetic play. Art would become a weapon in the class struggle, and the poet, in a way more immediate than ever before, would be "an unacknowledged legislator of the world"; the artist would now be writing "on the side of history" and would thereby attain a new importance for his art; and, in attempting to align himself with the proletariat in one form or another, the artist would be able to draw upon material more vitally "real" than ever before.

A second complication in the motives and intentions of the left-wing intellectuals is to be found in a paradox inherent in the idea of a left-wing revolution itself, the uneasy and often violent union of anarchist tendencies with the need for order, discipline, and dogmatic fixity. In England, this paradox took a variety of forms among the intellectuals; most notable, perhaps, was the mixture of irresponsibility and moral seriousness that were principal elements of the intellectuals' attachment to communism. There was a great deal of irresponsibility in the movement, much of which has been suggested already. Most obvious with Auden is the element of explosive nonsense and unbridled parody in some of the earlier poems and the high spirits of the later dramas; that this tendency manifested itself in a great deal of the left-wing art of the thirties is indicated by Symons when he notes that left-wing writing at its worst tended to break down into unentertaining nonsense on the one hand and propaganda on the other, a division paralleling our two categories of irresponsibility and dogmatization. Another factor tending toward irresponsible anarchism is the way in which the thirties represented an explosive release of the new in many areas of English culture and thought, for the extreme energy of such a release would contain of necessity elements of exuberant chaos. We see arising a new poetry, a new visual art, a new social theory, a new method of sociological research, and a new social grouping of intellectuals; the combination of optimism and naiveté involved indicate a sudden release of thought and action which, for some reason, has been able to occur apart from the scathing eye of the mind's responsible censor. But perhaps the most interesting form of irresponsibility in the thirties was something wholly modern: protest and moral outrage were closely allied with an exhibitionistic urge, something that takes place only in a society that gives special news coverage to a culture of protest in its midst. One thinks, at one extreme, of some of the descriptions given by an older and wiser Spender of the characters he encountered in Spain; there, among the visiting artists, Spender noted an extreme sensitivity to the fact that they were being publicized, that they were on display both for the sake of the cause and for the sake of their own egos. At the other extreme, there is the engaging impudence of tone in

Auden's early work; here the outrageous becomes a style to be exhibited and to be enjoyed for the very excess of its display.

Another opposing force is at work; colder critical reason and the sense of necessary limitations, temporarily overthrown, reassert their control once more in the form of the strict limitation of thought about permissible dogma, and moral fervor returns in the form of the neo-religious attitude many people had toward the Party, their sense of having been converted to something larger than themselves, in which they could immerse both their private conscience and their personal identity. Thus, for example, intellectuals often submitted to considerable anti-intellectual abuse in the course of Party meetings, during which the opinions of real proletarians were held up to them as somehow more genuine and correct. To be sure, the intellectuals did remain in a sense an elite, for the Party remained very conscious of their prestige and did not ask them to do menial labor; since the Party was very concerned with ideological elaboration, with theoretical polemics in the journals, and with establishing a left-wing culture in England, the intellectuals did have a specialized and gratifyingly important function to perform. But the myth of the superiority of the proletariat allowed the intellectuals to feel as if they were submitting themselves to something greater than their private egos.

One of the principal reasons why the thirties now seems to us to represent, in some sense, an especially fruitful age for the politically engaged artist is the way in which the opposed tendencies of anarchism and order were able to coexist. If one had only the anarchistic tendency, political display would lose all serious content, and one could not believe that anything concrete would be brought about by the upheaval; if one had only the tendency toward dogma, Party order, and discipline for immediate action, the movement would, as it did in the Spanish Civil War period, gradually lose its innocence and naive ardor and would, as the sacrifices to Party exigency became more and more real, begin to become morally grotesque for all but the absolutely dedicated. Instead, during the most vital years of the thirties, there existed a very rare kind of balance; it was a time when one felt one could unite private personality and energy with public action, when one could act within a real world of seemingly great moral significance and yet without the guilty and deadening burden of responsibility, when one could dedicate himself to a political movement and philosophy in a spirit of release, even of frivolity, without the sense of trapping himself in the process, of stifling his finer energies, and when one could feel that at last the brute backside of history was not so irrevocably turned on the subtle logic of the mind, *Geist* not so painfully superfluous to *Macht*. A more terse and critical summary of the balance between the hypothetical and the real is provided by George Orwell's comment that "the whole left-wing ideology, scientific and utopian, was evolved by people who had no immediate prospect of attaining power";[38] although the ideology was elaborated with the earnestness of a belief in the imminent dawn of communism, it remained a basically intellectual commitment, and, as such, was developed with all the speculative abstraction of pure theory.

[38] "Writers and Leviathan," in *Collected Essays* (London: Mercury Books, 1961), p. 429.

The movement's intensity of hope and lack of concrete power was no doubt not far removed from a state of despair, and it did end in the sickeningly guilty headache of an awakening to find that one had been deceived, or, worse, that one had deceived oneself; nevertheless, it is *not* correct to ascribe, with Wood, the activism to an underlying political and cultural nihilism, for, during the years in which the delicate balance was struck, the young intellectuals felt themselves not only to be alive but to be alive with a (correct) purpose.

Such a balance was not simply due to the internal organization and mood of the left wing, for there were also certain social conditions that had to prevail for it to be held; of these, two are most important. First is the fact that the government of the day was so stable as to absorb internal protest without having to resort to political persecution; as Renato Poggioli points out in *The Theory of the Avant-Garde*,[39] one needs a democratic tolerance for a full-fledged culture of protest to thrive. At the same time, the government was beset with enough problems for the left-wing critics to be able to foresee and believe in its doom; it seemed as if the capitalist system had at last come close to proving its bankruptcy and that the eventual downfall would come about without even the need for a violent shove, an armed revolution, so that there was no pressing need for the left-wing intellectual either to renounce the privileges of his own class or to commence overtly illegal or violent activity. The second factor that supported the

[39] Cambridge, Mass.: Belknap Press of Harvard University Press, 1968, p. 95.

growth of the English intellectual left wing was bound up with the nature of the capitalist crisis; though there was a severe economic problem within English society, it was the rise of fascism that seemed the most essential and literal threat to democracy. Fascism was already at work within English society, both in the form of the B.U.F. and in the Marxist interpretation of it as the nightmare and logical consequence of capitalism; thus, the growth of the fascist regimes in Europe during the thirties made the left-wing position seem ever more necessary and reputable, and it was the Spanish Civil War that brought the most popular support to the Party. As a result, the English left-wing movement had, in fascism, both a visible enemy and an inexhaustible fund for the characteristic rhetoric of unmasking, for the opportunity to reveal the government as both productive of fascist sensibility and in collusion with the fascists; the worst enemy, though, remained externalized, at a distance from England, allowing one the breathing space necessary for a culture of protest.

What relevance, it must now be asked, does this description of the forces at work behind the left-wing intellectuals of the thirties have for a study of Auden? Most clearly, it should explain just why Auden was regarded as a literary spokesman for a sizeable group of his contemporaries. First, just as the English radical intellectuals were both in rebellion against and yet intimately related to English society and traditions, Auden's fantasy was tendentiously brash yet not violently hate-ridden; there were many ways in which its eccentric tendentiousness was quite consonant with English manners. Similarly, Auden's fantasy marked a release of energy and novelty that broke the bonds of a tired Georgian rhetoric; it did so without doing a total demolition job on literary tradition or literary form. Second, just as a chief impulse for the radical intellectuals was the revolutionary assertion of the energy of youth against the established fixture of age, Auden's poetry managed to bring the dialectic of youth and age to bear on English politics. Third, just as radical politics in England marked a fusion of attempted self-realization and social action, Auden's verse was obsessed with the mixture of private material and public theme and, in its thematic fusion of psychoanalysis with politics, it argued for a revolution that effected both a change in society and a change in heart. Finally, just as irresponsibility and discipline existed simultaneously in radical English politics, coexisting in an atmosphere of partly practical, partly utopian ferment, so Auden's verse effected an odd fusion of extravagant fantasy and rational control which combined to form a literary tone consciously ambiguous about its own seriousness and reliability.

More important than defining why Auden came to be a spokesman for a significant group of intellectuals is the fact that the English political scene provided him with an atmosphere ideally suited to his poetic growth. As in Berlin, Auden encountered a world that seemed to realize in the public domain many of the characteristics of his private sensibility; once again the private and the public and the imaginative and the real seemed to be remarkably intertwined with one another. He could expand beyond the Mortmere circle and Mortmere themes without forfeiting either of the most important aspects of that world: in writing for the English radical family, he would still be writing for a kind of self-conscious literary in-group, and, in participating in the enthusiasm for social change, which in its structure and preoccupations seemed so closely to resemble those of his own imagination, he would be exploring how the imagination relates to social reality in ways akin to but far more subtle, complex, and significant than those implicit in the Mortmerian attacks against a partly real, partly mythologized university.

4. Experiments in Political Voice

That Auden was concerned with creating a new, more effectively public voice for his poetry and with exploring the ways in which imagination and social reality are intertwined is clear from a number of the poems in *Look, Stranger!* Most immediately interesting in this respect is Poem XXX, the birthday poem for Christopher Isherwood; the subject is the two authors' attempt to reevaluate, alter, and make publicly relevant the private imaginations and friendships that once produced extravagant Mortmerian fantasy. The poem opens with several delightful, relaxed stanzas:

> August for the people and their favorite islands.
> Daily the steamers sidle up to meet
> The effusive welcome of the pier, and soon
> The luxuriant life of the steep stone valleys,
> The sallow oval faces of the city
> Begot in passion or good-natured habit,
> Are caught by waiting coaches, or laid bare
> Beside the undiscriminating sea.

Lulled by the light they live their dreams of free-
dom;
May climb the old road twisting to the moors,
Play leap frog, enter cafés, wear
The tigerish blazer and the dove-like shoe.
The yachts upon the little lake are theirs,
The gulls ask for them, and to them the band
Makes its tremendous statements; they control
The complicated apparatus of amusement.[1]

The setting and many of its ornaments are part of the
gang's old shared myth-material; Isherwood describes the
original island in *Lions and Shadows*. More relevant is "The
Island," a short piece by Edward Upward, published nine
months before Auden's poem;[2] it also concerns the various
ways that one can "read" a resort island within a political
context, and it ends, much more heavy-handedly than does
Auden's poem, in a political moral. Upward's piece reveals
the major rhetorical possibility of such an island for a politically conscious writer; inside a setting designed for a
variety of indulgences, a setting in which the contemplating
mind has both leisure and freedom for meditation, in which
each interest can exist according to its taste, in pure loll
or athletic activity, what meaning does politics have? Or,
what is the relationship between private pleasure and political experience? Unlike Upward, who focuses completely
upon the resort town, drawing his political point finally
from contradictions inherent in the setting itself, Auden

[1] London: Faber and Faber, 1936, p. 63.
[2] In *The Railway Accident and Other Stories* (London: Heine-
mann, 1969), pp. 209–219.

does not draw his moral from the scene of the island; instead he uses the place to evoke the mood of leisure, the private hedonism which, he says, is the "people's" dream of freedom, and the diverse community of man at play, each attempting to live his dream in an artificial context, and only then does he go on to consider more abstractly the political evils of the time and their relationship to private indulgence.

With the fourth stanza, then, the poem shifts to a more direct consideration of its main theme; in the context of a birthday tribute to Christopher Isherwood, Auden describes their development away from their early fantasies, forms of enjoyment as private and as much tinged with mere wish-fulfillment as the enjoyment of the bathers. From the youthful hauteur of nine years previous in which only the "acid and austere" were praised but behind which lay a rather childish concern with ideas that were simultaneously "extraordinary and false" and from the sentimental faith in the healing powers of the word "love" of four years previous, Auden and Isherwood have weaned themselves; now, presumably, they are capable of grasping social reality in the full evil of its "hour of crisis and dismay," and the remedy is seen in Isherwood's new emotional and artistic maturity:

> What better than your strict and adult pen
> Can warn us from the colours and the consolations,
> The showy arid works, reveal
> The squalid shadow of academy and garden,
> Make action urgent and its nature clear?

The imaginations that created Mortmerian fun have grown

up, supposedly, into minds able both to define reality—the academy is no longer an unreal don, but a more substantial "squalid shadow"—and to prescribe the relevant curative action.

But all the time Auden is saying this, one senses the inadequacy of his statements; it is not only that one has very little faith that action will ever be urgent or its nature clear, but also that the words "crisis and dismay" do not seem, in the context of the poem, to be compelling. The stanzas in which the malaise of society is defined are a list of fantastic personifications:

> The close-set eyes of mother's boy
> Saw nothing to be done; we look again:
> See Scandal praying with her sharp knees up,
> And Virtue stood at Weeping Cross,
> The green thumb to the ledger knuckled down,
> And Courage to his leaking ship appointed,
> Slim Truth dismissed without a character,
> And gaga Falsehood highly recommended.
>
> Greed showing shamelessly her naked money,
> And all Love's wondering eloquence debased
> To a collector's slang, Smartness in furs,
> And Beauty scratching miserably for food,
> Honour self-sacrificed for Calculation,
> And Reason stoned by Mediocrity,
> Freedom by Power shockingly maltreated,
> And Justice exiled till Saint Geoffrey's Day.

At first these personifications seem to have a certain power; although they are only to a small extent specifically analytic of a social crisis, they seem forceful by virtue of Auden's ability to find witty modern images for moral abstractions. All sense of a serious reality behind these witty images, however, is dissipated when the list goes on in the second stanza; what might have been moral eloquence turns into Audenesque pyrotechnics, marvelously inventive, but there mainly for display and far from the ideal of a "strict and adult pen."

In the last stanza the mood changes again, and this time a much happier note is struck. The mood deepens into a calmness of thought and a tone of controlled private utterance, and Auden reaches one of the poem's loveliest images:

> And all sway forward on the dangerous flood
> Of history, that never sleeps or dies,
> And, held one moment, burns the hand.

The image does justice to the shift of mood; just as he has entered into a deeper calm, Auden has fashioned an image comprehensive not only of the whole harbor scene before him, but also of the concern that underlies all political effort, namely the attempt to relate oneself to the tide of history. This relationship is beautifully understated, and the lightness of the comedy involved in the idea of burning one's hand at a reactionary attempt to grab and halt history does not make the idea frivolous, but rather humanizes it, incorporates it in the warmth of a personal tone and the pleasure of comic rhetoric. The poem's critique of private pleasure—both on the beach and in self-indulgent art—and the advocacy instead of the asceticism of an art directly applicable to public reality were both simplistic;[3] here,

[3] It is interesting to note that, at about the same time he wrote

where a history oblivious to aesthetic enjoyment is nevertheless caught by it and where personal affection fuses with public theme, Auden's voice realizes itself most effectively.

It is no surprise that the volume's most important political poem is one which deals with the same questions in a far more consciously controlled way; Poem II, "Out on the lawn I lie in bed," considers the relationship of private pleasure and personal affection to public reality by means of a voice subtly critical of itself and of its relation, as imaginative language, to social reality. It has for its theme the meaning of private community in an unjust and imminently revolutionary world and can be described as Auden's dramatization of the feelings and attitudes of an enlightened liberal bourgeois, perhaps even a "fellow traveler." The community depicted in the poem is portrayed as having an almost haunting appeal; it is a place of leisure, of temporary stability and emotional release within a world of political disorder and injustice; it is deeply satisfying: within the private group each participant has, such as no one has in the anonymous and brutal public world, an identity. This small enclave of civility is seen in ironic juxtaposition to international despair, but here—as was not so in the early poems—this compromised position does not lead Auden to transform the speaker and his associates into figures of parody and to subvert the narrative voice of the poem; the speaker of the poem is fully aware of the dubi-

---

this poem, Auden qualified the assertion that poetry—even didactic poetry—should make "action urgent and its nature clear." See the Introduction to *The Poet's Tongue* as quoted in Monroe Spears, *The Poetry of W. H. Auden* (New York: Oxford University Press, 1968), pp. 88–89.

ous nature of his position, of the historical forces at work, and of the new world they will soon bring into being. As a member of a dying order, he sees clearly its injustices and foresees the order's and his own downfall, and, as a man of sympathetic vision, he—in the famous Auden synthesis of change of heart and political change, of Freud with Marx—sees how the downfall will bring about both social regeneration (will "calm / The pulse of nervous nations") and psychological rebirth into a genuine community and a new harmony with the past:

> May this for which we dread to lose
> Our privacy, need no excuse
>   But to that strength belong;
> As through a child's rash happy cries
> The drowned voice of his parents rise
>   In unlamenting song.[4]

The poem's mastery of a certain kind of rhetoric is what gives this revolutionary drama a feeling of great humanity and moral value; the beauties of both the prerevolutionary and postrevolutionary communities are portrayed with the fullest sympathy, instead of the former being scorned for the latter, as in doctrinaire propaganda. The mood of calm, contentment, and good fortune in a time and place hallowed by genuine friendship is realized fully at the beginning of the poem:

> Equal with colleagues in a ring
> I sit on each calm evening,
>   Enchanted as the flowers

---

[4] *Look, Stranger!*, p. 16.

> The opening light draws out of hiding
> From leaves with all its dove-like pleading
>   Its logic and its powers.

While the poetic rhetoric thoroughly establishes this magic of mood, it also introduces elements that criticize it; in this sense, the poem can be seen as a variation on Brecht's *Verfremdungseffekt*. At first, one notices not much more than a small clash in rhetoric; Vega is "conspicuous" overhead, an adjective which, in its coolness, prevents one from any release of poetic enthusiasm, and the detail that "my feet / Point to the rising moon" suggests a comic reevaluation of our attitudes toward moons on summer nights, attitudes often excessively romantic and literary. Instead, what emerges is something that seems very close to Auden's own character: a mild buffoonery in loveliness, which both accepts and criticizes his thorough enjoyment of the evening, the charms of nature, the witty companionship of cultivated society, and the ironies of the poem itself. This attitude is brought into even greater prominence in the sixth stanza:

> Now North and South and East and West
> Those I love lie down to rest;
>   The moon looks on them all:
> The healers and the brilliant talkers,
> The eccentrics and the silent walkers,
>   The dumpy and the tall.

The mood is as irresistibly lyric as Benjamin Britten's musical setting for the poem; but the phrase "The dumpy and the tall" calls for a comic reevaluation, something which Britten unfortunately does not realize in his music. This reevaluation does not break the mood; rather it makes a lyric which is thoroughly conscious of itself and which—in spite of and because of that consciousness—is given an additional modulation, that of a mood which is aware and even hedonistically appreciative of itself.

With the next four stanzas, the discordances in mood begin to reveal themselves as more serious than those of a clash in genre. The poem's very gentleness of tone is shown to be maintained at the expense of others; the "freedom in this English house" depends upon a deliberate refusal to contemplate the "doubtful act" that makes it possible, and "kindness to ten persons" is but kindness to ten and ridiculously inadequate in the face of mass suffering. Yet even this seriousness of discord does not destroy the lyric mood of the poem. Not only has the poetic mood been too fully evoked to be so quickly dispersed, but also part of the richness of the original mood was that of a consciousness able to perceive discord and still be both open and calm. As the discord grows in intensity, the balance becomes ever more precarious, but Auden avoids an explosion of mood and a discrediting of sentiment by turning now to the release of such inharmonious energy through revolution, a revolution seen as inevitable in that

> now no path on which we move
> But shows already traces of
> Intentions not our own. . . .

The revolution itself does not involve the utter discrediting of the group that foresees here its own overthrow. Unlike the enemies in the more tendentious poems, the members of this group do not become caricatures or gro-

tesques, to be cast out by a fantastic gesture; they experience and are changed by the upheaval. The upheaval, during which

> through the dykes of our content
> The crumpling flood will force a rent,
>   And, taller than a tree,
> Hold sudden death before our eyes
> Whose river-dreams long hid the size
>   And vigours of the sea[,]

will not simply lay waste but will create a new world, in
which the voice of the old—and therefore the voice of this
poem—will rise "In unlamenting song." The final note of
the poem is one of benediction and forgiving, a reestablish-
ment of harmony; one sees here a very full realization of
Auden's lifelong preoccupation with a love that includes
all that would spite it and that testifies to the value of individuals in a world that has radically undercut the ideal and
the fact of individuality.

An experienced reader of Auden will remain skeptical of
the poem for a number of reasons. Just as the magic of the
prerevolutionary group was undercut by a rhetoric im-
plicitly critical of that magic, our general knowledge of
Auden's self-consciousness about his own rhetorical mastery should make us critical of the fairly unqualified magic
of the poem's ultimate vision. Also, the role of the con-
scientious liberal-bourgeois is a poetic identity, only one of
many of Auden's partly serious, partly fictional poetic
roles; similarly, the group pictured in the poem may dis-
tantly echo the Mortmerian "gang" and the setting of a
momentary retreat found within a chaotic world is remi-

niscent of the second ode of *The Orators*, the land of farms into which newcomers are brought and initiated. The setting of the poem will be seen as depending not only on the poem itself, but rather as something interesting to Auden in and of itself, as one of a number of settings which recur regularly throughout his poetry and which are poetically "read" in different ways, ways which depend upon Auden's intellectual interest of the time; the number of such settings is large and comprises such divergent elements as varieties of landscape (of limestone, industrial decay, mountains, etc.), devices of perspective (of which an overhead view, be it from a hilltop or an airplane, is the favorite), and conceptions of the city, the garden, and the island. Not to recognize such a setting behind any individual poem will cause the critic to misjudge tones, misplace emphases, and to form, in general, a slightly incorrect view of how the rhetoric of that particular poem operates; it is as if Auden, as a poet who is at his richest in a free play of ideas in a poetic world in which all things are imminently suggestive of ideas and rhetoric, is aided by a recurring and, in a sense, stable group of poetic settings, into which he can integrate whatever intellectual preoccupations he may then have.

In addition to realizing that the setting of the poem and the speaking voice are as much conscious fictional devices that are played with for their own sakes as they are means toward the expression of a truth meant to criticize and transcend poetic fiction, we become aware that, as much as Auden is interested in making a political comment through the poem, he is involved, in a much more sheerly formal sense, in working out certain ideas, wittily and precisely, in the process of the poem. The synthesis of Freud and Marx is simultaneously a formal and a thematic interest, and, with Auden, the two interests remain almost always distinct and often slightly antagonistic to one another. Even more interesting is the fact that the end of the poem, the achievement of an inclusive synthesis by means of a rhetoric of humanistic benediction, is somewhat qualified by the fact that Auden is as much interested in the rhetoric of humanistic benediction as he is in the actual appearance of such a moment in the world; one need only think of how Wilfred Owen's statement that the "poetry is in the pity" was an early slogan for the Mortmere group and of how Owen himself became such a familiar god to them that they were on a first-name basis with him. But although, as always with Auden, feeling is also pose, the feeling and pose are here more tactfully realized and conditionally harmonized than in many of the early poems. What was, in the Mortmere world, parodic role-play is realized here without parodic retraction; instead, the final resolution is placed in the conditional context of a Utopian dream.

The poems discussed here do not, of course, provide an exhaustive account of the political poetry of *Look, Stranger!;* as always, Auden is continuing to experiment with a variety of ideas and poetic genres simultaneously, with an eye to their rhetorical possibilities. The volume comprises a multiplicity of genres; for example, the popular song turned to political use, the allegorical sestina, the short and compressed political lyric after the manner of Blake and Yeats, and the politicized love poem. Both the kind of social analysis and the political attitude vary from poem to poem; for example, "Here on the cropped grass of the narrow ridge

I stand" is, like the two poems discussed, a form of political meditation within an occasional setting, but, for its content, makes an analysis of the disasters of industrialization in terms of a failure of love; in the "Epilogue," a figure of pure fantasy, the "tall-hatted botanist," looms behind the city's destruction although, at the close, the poem modulates into an acceptance of man's condition; and "Brothers, who when the sirens roar" is an adaptation of the Mortmerian impulse toward tendentious caricature to a more strictly Marxist attitude and propagandistic purpose, which ends, contradictorily in tone, both in the true Mortmere style of casting out the unreal villains and (in the original version of the poem) on a note of Marxist earnestness, a pledge of solidarity with the proletariat.

The poems chosen for discussion, however, represent the most significant development in Auden's political poetry during these years. They achieve, at their best, what the Mortmere mode could not, namely both a personal tone and a significant public reference; and they open up possibilities for an interaction of imagination with reality that is far richer than Mortmere's fantastic, self-parodying subversion of the real, in that they work toward a rhetoric critically conscious of and yet tolerant of, amused by, and even reverent toward its own fictions.

The critical self-awareness that characterizes "Out on the lawn I lie in bed" is totally lacking in the theatrical productions of Auden and Isherwood. The Group Theatre, unlike the group portrayed in "Out on the lawn I lie in bed," never attains any significant social reference for its works and never gets beyond an essentially Mortmerian dialectic of fantasy and reality.

The Dog Beneath the Skin would seem to belie these assertions. As a short look at the play will confirm, it has for its theme the growth of Francis away from a Mortmerian fantasy role into the identity of a Marxist radical. Francis' hometown, Pressan Ambo, is pure Mortmere; it is a rural English hamlet with an idyllic quality reminiscent of a fairy tale but marked in reality by a partially concealed inner rottenness. Francis' assumption of the dog's identity, then, is similar to the "gang's" withdrawal into the Rat's Hostel, for he is simultaneously escaping from and engaged in observation and satire of the distortions of that society:

> As a dog, I learnt with what a mixture of fear, bullying, and condescending kindness you treat those whom you consider your inferiors, but on whom you are dependent for your pleasures. It's an awful shock to start seeing people from underneath. My diary was my greatest friend. I worked away at it, like a scientist, polishing, punctuating, searching for the exact epithet, devoting months and even years to each one of you, noting every gesture, every intonation. I even managed to take photographs to illustrate my records, and very remarkable some of them are.
>
> And then, slowly, the horror and the pseudo-scientific interest began to wear off, too. I was growing older. I began to feel that I had been foolishly wasting my time. Hadn't it all been just a romantic escape, I asked myself? Wasn't it Life I was afraid of, hiding in my dog-skin? I think that, soon, I should have gone

away anyhow. But, as it happened, Alan Norman was chosen. I'd always liked him and so I took the opportunity of leaving when I did.[5]

Francis' decision to give up the identity of the dog for that of the political activist represents the culmination of whatever action the play has; his decision represents not only the casting off of his dog skin, the rejection of satirical withdrawal, but also the exposing of Pressan once and for all as anything but a fairy-tale world. Similarly, the idea that holds all the episodes together is that of a quest ending in the inversion of the traditional fairy-tale goal; instead of Alan's having done Pressan a service and having won thereby the hand of its princess, he finds that the princess is about to be married to a well-known munitions manufacturer and that Pressan is utterly ungrateful for his services. This theme is foreshadowed in the introductory semi-choruses, which evoke the young men in Pressan tossing in their beds:

> Their pillows do not comfort
>   Their uneasy heads.
> The lot that decides their fate
>   Is cast to-morrow,
> One must depart and face
>   Danger and sorrow.

[5] Auden and Isherwood, *Two Great Plays* (New York: Vintage, 1937), p. 108, reprinted by permission of Faber and Faber, Ltd., and Random House, Inc.; copyright, 1935, by The Modern Library Inc.; copyright 1937, by Random House. Isherwood's participation is not discussed because, according to Isherwood, the play derived mainly from Auden (*Exhumations* [London: Methuen, 1966], p. 12).

Of course it is nonsense that *this* quest involves anyone in serious danger and sorrow; it is characteristic of *Dog*, as it is characteristic of Auden's early work, that the most serious and elevated rhetoric coexists with the most unserious matter. With the close of the introductory chorus, we are back again to the purest of Mortmerian nonsense, that of figures both essentially contentless and unspeakably sinister, figures we encounter "with a wholly pleasing fictional fear";[6]

> The bolt is sliding in its groove
> Outside the window is the black removers van
> And now with sudden swift emergence
> Comes the woman in dark glasses and the hump-
>   backed surgeons
> And the scissor man.

Exactly what this warning, spoken by the leaders of the two semi-choruses (who identify themselves successively as the "clock" and "the guardians of the gate in the rock"), means is of course not clear; spoken by the representatives of the "town," it presumably turns on Pressan some of the Old Mortmerian rhetoric and exposes a threatening, psycho-surreal evil behind the apparent calm:

> We've been watching you over the garden wall
> For hours.

[6] Auden, *A Certain World* (New York: Viking, 1970), p. 53. The scissor man is taken from Dr. Hoffmann's *Struwelpeter*, from a poem which Auden glosses as about "masturbation, which is punished by castration." In Auden's chorus, however, this possible meaning for the scissor man is neither particularly clear, nor necessary, nor nearly so important as the effect.

> The sky is darkening like a stain,
> Something is going to fall like rain
> And it won't be flowers.

Thus, while Francis and Alan will emerge at the end as real men committed to the struggle against the system of which Pressan is only a part, Pressan itself is trapped in the world of the fairy tale gone sour; at the end of the play, the townspeople, in a stroke of farcical magic, are turned into beasts, a technique of sudden revelation and casting out reminiscent of the *J'en appelle*.

The difficulties with the play should be clear by now. In being so easily cast out, the world of Pressan Ambo shows itself as belonging to an earlier variety of enemy, one that was so unreal it would disappear when its bluff was called; as such, its public reference is minimal, and one is only unsettled to see, emerging triumphant from it, characters who claim for themselves a genuine public reference. Indeed, it would be far more consistent and satisfying to have Alan and Francis remain within the Mortmere world and to have their eventual declaration of opposition parodied; the final choosing up of sides would have been more effective if it had recognized and parodied its own infantile analogue, the choosing up of sides for, say a public-school rugger match.

Neither *The Ascent of F6* nor *On the Frontier* represent any improvement on *Dog*; in many ways, they prove to be far less effective. *The Ascent of F6* is, if anything, a deeper regression into the Mortmere mode; it is wholly fantastic in style and in theme represents a return to the politically ambiguous private mythology of the T. E. Lawrence hero-figure. *On the Frontier* is far more sober and publicly accessible; it is, however, a fairly thin, perfunctory drama, the greater discipline of its fantasy having been offset by no positive virtues. There are several reasons why the drama of Auden and Isherwood did not keep pace with the development in Auden's poetry.

The chief artistic motive of the drama is a particularly conscious sort of fun. *Dog* is a political revue, sophisticated in much of its satire, in its language, and in its ironic self-consciousness of form, the reworking and criticism of the naive fairy-tale quest; correspondingly, it relies for success upon the sophistication of its performance. The play must be done with virtuosity, so that the audience will be entertained despite themselves, despite the fact that they are aware of all the tricks and the show; what one finally appreciates most is the play's pace, its stylistic tricks, its flair for witty gesture rather than concern for what the gesture may signify, for the play depends not so much upon the development of any weight of meaning as on how well each part of it "works." It would be very difficult to reconcile such a form with any serious didacticism, and, though *Dog* pretends to be didactic, it effects no reconciliation of fun with didactic message. What Auden has done is not to make a message more accessible by making it palatable; instead, through the drama's very virtuosity, through its fast pace, its wealth of ornament, its stylistic novelty and theatrical effectiveness—in short, through its very exhibitionism of fantasy and virtuosity, Auden is trying to dazzle his audience first and only secondarily confront them with the moral that all this dazzle ostensibly serves. Auden's theatre nickname, Uncle Wiz, is thus very apt; it suggests the mock-sorcery involved in turning a didactic purpose into virtuoso entertainment and thus an ambiguous attitude toward that didactic purpose. On the one hand, the sorcery is only mock-sorcery, and one cannot forget the didactic message altogether; on the other hand, one tries as much as possible to remove that didacticism from the realm of the straightforward, flat statement by transforming it into something as stylistically alive as possible. This solution reflects a major dilemma for the artist–fellow traveler who is not willing to sacrifice his art altogether to politics; although he wants to be politically relevant, to commit himself by submitting his art to a political theme and perhaps even use, he reasserts his art and his artist's superiority by the practically destructive virtuosity of the form he gives that message. That Auden's political drama should have regressed to a tendentious, private indulgence in the fantasy of Mortmere at the same time that it claimed for itself a larger political reference and didactic point can be related as well to the groupishness of the aptly named Group Theatre. When one's identity as a member of a small community comes to rest less upon a sense of a group than it does on the sense of an in-group, an exuberance and a conscious delight in the irresponsibility of that exuberance, the fact that it ultimately denies any connection with the outside world, becomes one's chief motive force; this enthusiastic suspension of reality and social identity is finally antagonistic to the demands of a politicized conscience, which would attempt to apply an energy which is, by definition, solipsistic. Although the sheer high spirits of such enthusiasm can, given the audacious, exhibitionistic magic of an Uncle Wiz, occasionally carry us away with them, they can only do so at moments; but, as a comment by Isherwood indictaes, the Group Theatre provided enough of these moments to make its productions successful occasions:

> By the time Auden returned from Spain, *F.6* had already started its run. So he had not been present at the rehearsals, in the course of which Rupert Doone, our director, had made several changes with my full approval. The night I went with Auden to see the play, he turned to me, a few minutes after the curtain had gone up, and said in a loud reproachful whisper, '*My dear*, what have you *done* to it?' The theatre was tiny and most of the audience heard this, with vast amusement.[7]

Auden's description of the form of the "Letter to Lord Byron" is not only an apt description of the "Letter" but also of the mood of the whole travel book, *Letters from Iceland:*

> I want a form that's large enough to swim in,
>   And talk on any subject that I choose,
> From natural scenery to men and women,
>   Myself, the arts, the European news:
>   And since she's on a holiday, my Muse
> Is out to please, find everything delightful
> And only now and then be mildly spiteful.[8]

The form of the "Letter" is indeed large enough to swim

---

[7] *Exhumations*, p. 11.

[8] Auden and Louis MacNeice, *Letters from Iceland* (New York: Random House, 1937), p. 21.

in, and the relish with which Auden swims indicates how writing such verse represents for him both a comic hedonism (he is conscious of the overtones of "swim") and a hedonistic comedy (to swim so humorously is clearly a grand pleasure). A large part of this pleasure stems from the fact that the verse allows Auden to "talk on any subject that I choose," and the absolute freedom of talk satisfies an important side of Auden's character, a kind of intellectual frivolity that operates in a realm between that of chat and that of thought, the realm of lively opinion. Auden is a man of an astounding variety of opinions, not all of which are necessarily in harmony with each other, and one feels that the very act of holding and expounding an opinion is for him a self-sufficient pleasure; there would be, moreover, a sense of marvelous freedom in an occasion in which one could, relishing his own semicomic intractibility and oddity of mind, simply talk, talk, talk. It is difficult to guess exactly how important a part of Auden is this semicomic but almost physical gusto for opinions and relish in the pose of being opinionated, but perhaps we can remain content with an oblique hint; insofar as, on holiday, one feels he can at long last be himself and then proceeds to relax and be that self for a little while, to this extent we can take Auden to be, in writing the "Letter," at last himself. It is a rare and enlivening pleasure to be able to express oneself in the range circumscribed by the emotions of delight and spite, of high spirits and equally spirited minor releases of venom, but, as with the ordinary vacationer, one can only do it so long before one just has to get back to the office again. Auden is, even more than the other members of his gang, an expert on the theory and practice of holidays and can carry this tone with just the right balance between the stale misery of feeling that it has been *only* an escape and the too heady overestimation of its having been more of a fulfillment than it really was; as a result, *Letters from Iceland* turns out to be an exceptionally refreshing and enjoyable literary holiday, for both critic and poet.

The tone of satire of "Letter to Lord Byron" is of a particular sort and is as much dictated by the form of the verse as it is by the occasion; the discovery of a Byronic voice was for Auden a stroke of very good fortune,[9] and to have such good fortune is itself a part of both the verse and the holiday.[10] A stanza of this sort must be characterized by kaleidoscopic speed and verbal dazzle, a dazzle both ludicrous and startling; Auden himself describes the technique in an essay on Byron:

> Neo-classical satire presupposes that the City of Man owes allegiance to certain eternal laws that are known to human reason and conscience; its purpose is to demonstrate that the individual or institution attacked violates these laws out of presumption, malice, or stupidity. Satire of the Byronic kind presupposes no such

[9] Auden's rendition of the Byronic voice is aided by the fact that he addresses his letter to Lord Byron; he is thus able to make a more unrestrained use of the form, for, along with an appropriate tone, he has found an apt address for the poem, one that brings its derivative character into full display and that frees therefore the imitative faculty for as great an exhibition as possible.

[10] The stanza Auden uses is Rime Royal and not Byron's Ottava Rima, but both are a game for Auden to play; moreover, in not choosing "The proper instrument on which to pay / My compliments" (p. 22), Auden is living up to the spirit of Byron, that of, as Auden puts it, not accepting conventional "pieties as binding."

fixed laws. It is the weapon of the rebel who refuses to accept conventional laws and pieties as binding or worthy of respect. Instead of speaking in the name of all well-educated and sensible people, it speaks in the name of the individual whose innocence of vision has not been corrupted by education and social convention. . . . The structure and regular formality of the couplet, therefore, will never do for this variety of satire; the sort of verse that it needs is what may be termed, though not pejoritively, doggerel-verse, that is to say, in which the element of chance in language seems to predominate over the elements of fate and choice.[11]

Similarly, Auden's verse depends upon the element of chance, both in its sound and in jumping out to catch the next good effect or idea and then jumping as quickly on to the next; it is a verse without fixed points for meditation and this lack of fixity allows no dawdling on ideas. What carries the satire is a posture of rebellion against all that is conventionally pious; its principal tone is irreverence and the most consistent target of the "Letter" is best summarized by the words "normality" and "status quo." Auden is being a rebel for the cause of eccentricity; as he says in the letter to Isherwood, distinguishing them from the "Scandinavian sanity" of Iceland, "the truth is, we are both only really happy living among lunatics."[12] Thus, in the "Letter," normality becomes the "Goddess of bossy under-

[11] "The Life of That-There Poet," *The New Yorker*, 34 (April 26, 1958), 135–136.
[12] Auden and MacNeice, p. 30.

lings," whose state, Reality, is totalitarian;[13] in the second section of the "Letter," where the most comprehensive social analysis is given, those who serve Normality, the dragon of law and order, in terror and abjection become defenders of that which will

> In every age rear up to defend
> Each dying force of history to the end.[14]

This idea is not unique to the "Letter," for one of Auden's favorite opinions has been that neurosis itself has a positive value, both in terms of private character and social betterment; in the "Letter," though, this contention is expressed with unusual vigor and argumentativeness. Indeed, in many ways the "Letter to Lord Byron" represents one of the most appealing voices of the thirties; its lightness and irreverence frees it from being dated in its opinion or oppressive in its sentiment and allows it to express fully the thirties' anarchistic wealth of new ideas, its vigorous optimism in the midst of an equally vigorous forecast of social doom, and its youthful and exhibitionistic rebellion against the status quo.

In many ways, this voice would seem to smack of the parodic irresponsibility of the plays; it would thus be without significant social reference and would, in its manner, be close kin to the Mortmerian parodic subversion of reality by fantastic invention. The inventiveness and irresponsibility of the "Letter," however, are tempered and focused in a number of ways; what Auden has done is find a mode in which private indulgence and public accessibility and fan-

[13] Ibid., p. 207.
[14] Ibid., p. 58.

tasy and reality can come together without denial of either side. Since the poem is a Byronic holiday, balancing the energy of escape with an awareness of the limited nature of that energy, it allows a tendentious imaginative frivolity which assumes a traditional social and literary role and yet works to criticize traditional society; and it finds a form in which reality and myth ultimately meet and complement with one another, blending into a voice of irreverent eccentricity.

That the vacation was in Iceland was essential to the vigorous balance of this poetic voice. Iceland had, for Auden, a peculiar sort of magic:

> In my childhood dreams Iceland was holy ground; when, at the age of twenty-nine, I saw it for the first time, the reality verified my dream; at fifty-seven it was holy ground still, with the most magical light of anywhere on earth.[15]

The magic was due in part to Auden's love of the sagas, fostered by his father, who read them to him as a child, and in part to his own sense of his Icelandic ancestry; it manifested itself throughout his early poetry in the form of the sagas' literary influence and in the recurring symbol of the island. From the start, Iceland is a fusion of the real and the fictional; the term "holy ground" is to a certain extent misleading, redolent of the mellowness of retrospection,[16] for the tone of the place and the happiness it inspired

---

[15] Auden and MacNeice, *Letters from Iceland* (London: Faber and Faber, 1965), p. 8. I shall refer to this edition as *Letters* (1965).

[16] The tone of the introduction to the later edition is so much

were of a different order to the Auden of age twenty-nine.

Iceland should be seen as representing a kind of idyll for Auden; as a society in miniature, it fulfilled the principal requirement for an idyll, that it be experienced within a time and place that are limited, distinct from the rest of the world, and somehow complete in themselves. The tone of Auden's presentation of the island indicates that for him an idyllic setting is of a distinctive kind; it is one in which there is also a strong element of the fantastic and the ludicrous. Iceland is filled with gratuitous comedy; utterly unimportant to the world, so socially ingrown that it represents both a real society and an Audenesque gang, incurably provincial and thus a source of constant anthropological amusement, in a wretched climate, not producing anything, and made out of volcanoes which, even when they explode, are less tragic than farcial, due to the contrast between the vast scale of the disorder with the purely local quality of its effects, Iceland is the occasion for much wryness. To be an adventurer come to Iceland, for example, is to be a little bit absurd, for what the devil is there to be found in Iceland? Auden and MacNeice amuse themselves greatly with quotations from travel literature, an amusement that comes at the comic expense of both Iceland and her explorers; particularly delightful is the testament of

An inarticulate Wordsworthian
   "I wish it were in my power, Sir, to give you such a description of this place as it deserves, but I fear mine

---

one of mellow retrospection that it seems that Auden is not just mellow, but also enjoying the portrayal of himself as such.

will always remain inferior in point of expression. So much is certain, at least, Nature never drew from anyone a more cheerful homage to her Great Creator than I here paid him.'[17]

As one reads, one begins to get the impression that, despite the testimony of Pliny Miles, Iceland is not altogether real; one only has to read the account of the 1890 Revolution to feel that one is living in a world of caricature rather than of reality.

Although Iceland was a privately significant mythic place, Auden was able to integrate it into the public world.

Though writing in a 'holiday' spirit, its authors were all the time conscious of a threatening horizon to their picnic—world-wide unemployment, Hitler growing every day more powerful and a world-war more inevitable. Indeed, the prologue to that war, the Spanish Civil War, broke out while we were there.[18]

This background surfaces at a number of places in the book; at the same time Iceland is the place Auden and Mac-Neice chose for their holiday,

The Nazis have a theory that Iceland is the cradle of the Germanic culture. Well, if they want a community like that of the sagas they are welcome to it. I love the sagas, but what a rotten society they describe, a society with only the gangster virtues.[19]

The comment here is unusually strident in tone; the more

[17] *Letters*, p. 72.
[18] *Letters* (1965), p. 8.
[19] *Letters*, p. 119.

predominant note of satire reminds us of the way Hitler and his whole notion of Nazi culture were seen as farcical, a joke in supremely bad taste. The very fact that Auden and MacNeice can be so delighted by Iceland and can discover in it so much of the ludicrous becomes a technique for exposing the Nazis as Malvolios, utterly blind to the real nature of the island, blind to its humanities, standing cross-gartered in their *Deutschtum*, and grinning out at each other through their close-set German blue eyes, the only difference between them and Malvolio being the fact that they have power as well as egotism. To make their point, Auden and MacNeice need only to title a picture of an appealingly earnest little boy "Germanischer Typus."

The comically absurd idyll of Iceland has been used to expose both a particular political target and, in general, a reality that has become fixed, humorless, and therefore inhuman. The tendentious use of an idyll, one comically conscious of its own unreality, its fictional status as an Arcadian societal dream, is one of Auden's surest resources as a political poet: we have seen it loom behind the edenic Mortmere "gang," the group in "Out on the lawn I lie in bed," and, now, Iceland. The chief difference between these three uses of an Arcadian idyll lies not only in the nature of the idyll itself, but also in the way in which it is tendentiously used: the first tended normally toward a parody-apocalypse; the second culminated in a humanistic Marxist revolution; and the third retained its holiday irresponsibility, using it as a basis for widespread commentary. That this third voice is the most satisfying indicates something important about Auden: for his social criticism, the Arcadian impulse is more important than the utopian dream, and it thus comes as no surprise that, after his conversion, Auden will write more explicitly from the standpoint of a confirmed, yet self-critical Arcadian, as in "In Praise of Limestone" and "Vespers."

Auden's trip to Spain was not quite so much of a holiday; he went, wrote one dispatch, returned, and published a poem, never mentioning the trip thereafter. The journey remains shrouded in the spurious tales that grew up about it, stories like that of Auden's participation as an ambulance driver; one report on his activities, however, is worth citing, for, even though it is not firmly substantiated, it seems, given our general impression of Auden, most plausible. Claud Cockburn describes Auden's visit in a perfectly appropriate tone, a tone that makes us suspect, even in the face of our better knowledge, that Claud Cockburn is not real:

> Quite a lot of the literary people of the '30s had an exaggerated idea of physical action. They discovered in Spain that every Tom, Dick and Harry who knew the innards of a bren-gun was better at it than them; then came disillusionment which could easily lapse over into a feeling that the whole thing was no good. They were always thinking I must *act*, I must *do* something, but the poets' effectiveness, in their most political actions, was nil. At the outset Auden had the feeling that life could not be carried on at all without some kind of union with the party. So he came to Spain; of course, what we really wanted him for was to go to the front, write some pieces saying hurrah for the Republic, and then go away and write some poems,

also saying hurrah for the Republic; and that would be his job in the war—and bloody important at that. Instead of which, unfortunately, he took the whole thing terribly seriously; he wanted to *do* something.

I was mixed up in this because by some awful mischance it was taken for granted that I knew the aims and objectives of any Anglo-American who sought a visa for Spain. When Auden came out we got a car laid on for him and everything. We thought we'd whisk him to Madrid and that the whole thing would be a matter of a week before the end-product started firing. But not at all: the bloody man went off and got a donkey, a mule really, and announced that he was going to walk through Spain with this creature. From Valencia to the Front. He got six miles from Valencia before the mule kicked him or something and only then did he return and get in the car to do his proper job.[20]

The combination of a voiced seriousness of intention, Auden's participation in the general desire to do something, with a willful eccentricity of behavior smacking of the holiday spirit of the Iceland trip (where he had enjoyed traveling on the Icelandic ponies), and of a parody of a symbolic pilgrimage, sound very much like Auden; they

[20] "A Conversation with Claud Cockburn," *The Review*, 11–12 (1964), p. 51. Auden's most recent statement about his trip to Spain makes, however, no reference to these incidents: "I just wandered about in Barcelona and Valencia. They didn't give me anything to do—perhaps because I wasn't a party member." (Alan Levy, "In the Autumn of the Age of Anxiety," *The New York Times Magazine*, August 8, 1971, p. 42.)

also suggest some reasons why he would not have talked about his trip on his return. Probably for the first time Auden's attempt to confront a political situation with humorous extravagance and his desire to do something as a literary man were both frustrated, or, worse, they showed themselves to be out of place among "men of action"; he was limited to filling his role of poetical propagandist as quickly and efficiently as possible. The result, however, was the most satisfactory poem anyone wrote about the Spanish Civil War.

Instead of evoking the heroism, nobility, and tragic death of fighters for the Spanish Republic or instead of trying in some other way to give the events of the war some particularly "poetic" character or particularly appalling grotesqueness, Auden's "Spain 1937" evokes what seems to be the full range and variety of human life and history, a life and history that accent their ordinariness by containing more than a fair share of the trivial and absurd. The emphasis is upon all the various human things that happen within the flow of time and which would be happening in just as greatly disconnected profusion today if it were not for Spain's crisis; to capture this sense of profusion, Auden draws on a great wealth of detail and of ideas and finds a variety of rhetorics in which to embody them, and, contrary to what one would expect, the lists do not often become flat or chaotic. The brilliance of the rhetoric and the finesse with which different rhetorical forms are mixed makes most details in the lists entertaining (and, thus, apparently significant) in and of themselves.

The rhetorical mastery of "Spain" cannot be too much emphasized; provides the poem's abstract structure with an animating spirit. The local effects provide a flow of enjoyment; the oratorical structure provides a direction of movement and gives the poem the sense of having been, for all the incongruities, elevated and even noble; and several abstract ideas give the poem as much structural argument as necessary. Out of history's mass of engaging detail and out of profusion of the private purposes of artist or scientist emerges an intellectual drama; nations "combine each cry" and invoke the "life / That shapes the individual belly and orders / The private nocturnal terror," a life that is, then, a combination of genetics, evolution, and psychology, in short, a comprehensive version of a shaping life force. What the nations want to be able to do is to regress into prayer, to appeal to this unconscious natural force to civilize their lives as it orders robins into "plucky canton[s]" or creates the "vast military empires of the shark" or, by extension perhaps, forges cruel, regressive Germans into *Volk;* be it in the form of God's dove or Freud's "furious papa" or technology's "mild engineer," the life force should descend and save.[21]

The life gives, as well it should, a negative response to this plea and defines itself thereby in an important manner. Life's answer is to put man back upon his own powers of choice, his own conscious morality, for life is "whatever you do" and it embodies itself in all aspects of one's activity, no matter how trivial, from the humorous story to one's business voice to one's marriage. The vision is in one sense profoundly optimistic; it presupposes that the paradise envisioned by Marx is now possible, that at least man has re-

[21] Auden, *Spain* (London: Faber and Faber, 1937), p. 9.

moved himself from the pressure of necessity and can, if he so wants, control his fate. The choices are moreover clear; in Spain's finality of focus, they turn out to be basically two, two choices that emerge from all the data of recorded history in the sense that a turning point in history emerges from the random diffusion of yesterdays and tomorrows. One can either choose the "just city" or choose the "suicide pact, the romantic / Death."

Thus we have the theoretical justification for Auden's evocation of life in all its randomness and from all its different walks; in Spain, one finds a finality of historical choice, standing out from centuries of detail like a rock from a stream. It is in Spain that one must fight his own private battle for private harmony; the choice is as deeply personal as it is social and public.

> On that arid square, that fragment nipped off from
>   hot
> Africa, soldered so crudely to inventive Europe;
>   On that tableland scored by rivers,
> Our thoughts have bodies; the menacing shapes of
>   our fever
> Are precise and alive.

The closing stanzas present the other side to the poem's optimism; the power to shape one's own environment according to what one chooses is an awful power, one that places a burden of moral weight upon man and that isolates him from the natural world. For the just cause of Spain, he must accept both the "deliberate increase in the chances of death" and the "conscious acceptance of guilt in the necessary murder"; in doing so, he faces a world where

The stars are dead. The animals will not look.
We are left alone with our day, and the time is
    short, and
    History to the defeated
May say Alas but cannot help or pardon.

The conclusion is, given certain dogmas about Spain, optimistic; the lines are an exhortation to act and make the promise that, if one is successful in Spain, one becomes fully human, and one makes the just city. There is, though, pathos in a detail like "The animals will not look"; man is alone. The poem becomes, despite all its conscious, managed brilliance and intentionally humorous discords, *almost* moving.

Now there are many ways in which one can object to "Spain 1937."

"I don't care what you say," remarks an accuser worried most by the poetics of the thing. "The structure *is* arbitrary; why Auden can just throw any old thing into it."

"Yes, *Auden* can," comes the answer, with meaningful emphasis.

Or, from another standpoint, the critic or poet obsessed with the fusion of passion and politics, poetry and history: "What is regrettable, really regrettable, is the way the man lacks all personal involvement in what he says. The whole thing is abstract and manipulated, when *men* are out there *dying!* If the best he can come up with is a line like "Fumbled and unsatisfactory embrace before hurting," why he is more of a comic-strip writer than a poet, for not only does he not feel, but his dramatizations are crude and clichéd. And, now that I think of it, I've hit on a general principle:

every time one does not feel (and feel authentically) his response is trite, managed, crude, and above all clichéd. That, that's the trouble with your poet."

A not very temperate answer would be: "But my dear man, you miss what Auden is trying to do. He isn't, after all, as he himself implies, writing a political *Liebestod*, a *Liebestod* in the medium not of sex but of righteousness. Nor is he trying to write anything like trench romanticism, be it trite or immediate, nor is he trying to give one the very scent of battle or the sight of victims of history strung out upon the barbed wire. Nor is he trying to give us a Swiftian denunciation of the fascists, of course carefully doctored so that it doesn't, as Swiftian denunciations tend to do, damn our guys as well. Auden is, in contrast, a rationalist, and as such is concerned simultaneously with Spain as both particular incident and as idea, as exemplum. The theme of the poem is consciousness of choice, and the implication is that only when one accepts this consciousness of choice can one really progress toward the "just society"; why should he write a poem that is meant to poeticize war or to daemonize a political movement? Also—and I don't believe I'm stretching the point too much here—one can argue that the particular irreverence and detachment of tone which no doubt lies behind your distaste for the poem, along with the fact that many of the images play upon the trite, upon preformed images we have of the world, one can argue that these very things serve to increase our consciousness. The fumbled embrace works not only to invoke a modestly poignant vision of love's inability to express itself in times of war, but also to invoke the fact that it is only a conception of battle, something which many poetic images, in their enthusiasm to seize life by the throat, seek to suppress. In playing on an explicitly popular conception of battle, something we have encountered in all the movies, it raises the question as to how true our conceptions of experience are, for it is brought home to us how many of our feelings about things stem from such popular archetypes."

Our accuser is probably not at all satisfied with this answer; even if he would assent to it, there would still remain alive (and all the more so for the sake of being frustrated) a certain intensity of desire to censure, what one feels in the face of someone who both uses language and evokes emotions too easily for our taste and who therefore remains both untrapped by what he has said and capable of saying almost anything. This is a curious prejudice; it is interesting to note that one feels often more moral outrage against people like Auden than one does against people who actually do bad things. Our accuser casts about for still another way to quash Auden:

"I hate to limit my censure to the poem and not be able to reach the man behind it. But it's a start. The poem is false."

"Yes indeed. He's writing a propaganda poem, of course (and it's a good one, don't you think?); he's doing it both for the sake of his own reputation and to fulfill what was expected of him by his group, that of concerned English left-wing intellectuals who had helped in gathering about this issue the largest popular support that any English left-wing cause had ever had. Auden's poem is better than the poems of the other English intellectuals who wrote about Spain; it carries its didacticism more adeptly (even though this adeptness infuriated those who didn't believe that their pamphlets were flat and ephemeral) and it had more to say of a general nature than did most. Of course, Auden should and does feel bad about plumping for 'necessary murder' and, in the last stanza, 'equating,' as he puts it, 'goodness with success.' But one feels that the motive behind this ruefulness is not just the shock at finding out that he had advocated an immoral doctrine but also the embarrassment of having advocated it in service of a cause that turned sour toward the end, revealing the more unpleasant aspects of political involvement; the embarrassment of having been swept along with the general flow would have been acute for Auden, who, although he had a penchant for and drew much poetic material and even 'inspiration' from small literary groups, had seldom sacrificed his individuality to these groups and generally came to dominate the others in them. Indeed, most of the others were just as blindly caught up in the left-wing drama as was Auden, and most were not only just as false about it, but also clumsier and more tedious in their expression of that falseness; of those few who might perhaps have had the right to condemn Auden, most died in Spain and thus became inarticulate. Only Orwell drubbed him solidly for it, but nobody important listened to Orwell in those days."

"Good. It strikes me that one can go from here to a general condemnation of Auden, which would be an admirable thing. If he could write such a good propaganda poem, and, as you say, write it *as* propaganda, because it was the *thing to do* then, would this not mean that his poetic skills themselves lie in the *direction* of propaganda, that to do a bad thing so well indicates a certain, well, *deficiency* in *character.* . . ."

And with this we are back to many of the persistent doubts critics have felt for years about Auden's poetry. Nor are these doubts quite so unfounded in the case of "Spain 1937" as the little dialogue would seem to suggest; indeed, the "we" of the dialogue were not above some rather insensitive rhetoric. In crudest form, the exchange represents an exchange between the Prig and the Accomplice, and it seemed wise to give the latter a bit more than his due, because he has been so often slighted in the past. The point to be made is that a poem like "Spain 1937" divides our mind in much this way. On the one hand, there is part of us that knows the sentiment is false, but wants nevertheless to play along, because the poem is so entertainingly verbal and so apparently effortless in its construction and because our complicity allows us two very attractive pleasures: pleasure in an irreverence that disregards Proper Feeling and a certain aristocratic pleasure in the false, pleasure in the way the poem transforms—at times comically, at times almost elegantly—event into rhetoric, feeling into a conscious display of language, and being into verbal form. On the other hand, there resides still in each of us the Prig, that which feels compelled to call a Spade a Spade and thus to put the damn poem in its place. If the Prig is commonsensical, he may object to Auden's cavalier treatment of dying men; if the Prig is more sophisticated, he may very effectively attack Auden as having written a tasteless poem. But even in the latter case the Prig cannot extricate himself fully from his moralist's heavy-handedness; the fact that it is poetic language that is being judged, not deeds, makes the claim of the Accomplice, the verbal *Mitspieler*, impossible to ignore.

That the "prig" and the "accomplice" can never come to agreement about "Spain 1937" is a measure of the poem's failure. "Spain 1937" does not find a voice in which myth and reality successfully interrelate with one another; even though Auden may point up his rhetoric as fictional at the same time he is using it, the poem's chief source of pleasure lies in the ease with which historical event becomes rhetorical and not in the moral intensity with which that rhetoric is criticized. Similarly, the voice of "Spain 1937" is one in which the private pleasure derived from its rhetoric is not reconcilable with its public purpose; its verbal elegance sits only uneasily with the didactic intention, for the former implies a self-gratifying consciousness that, despite all claims to the contrary, is incompatible with the vulgar historical world of boring pamphlets and crude action.

"Spain 1937" is not atypical of Auden; it embodies a number of qualities noted throughout this study. "Spain 1937" shows Auden's facility with rhetoric, his enjoyment of writing against arbitrary structures, against a given body of rules as to subject and form, and his play with ideas taken from outside sources. These are also qualities of poets in general, but with Auden they have a special significance, something that can be illustrated by one of Auden's own distinctions, one between

> the visionary and the entertainer, the first being one who extends our knowledge of, insight into, and power of control over human conduct and emotion, with-

out whom our understanding would be so much the poorer. . . . Nor is entertainment an unworthy art: it demands a higher standard of technical achievement and a greater lack of self-regard than the average man is prepared to attempt. There have been many writers of excellent sensibility whose work is spoilt by a bogus vision which deprives it of the entertainment value which it would have had.[22]

Auden is himself a bizarre mixture of the two types of poets he distinguishes here, types fundamentally opposed to one another. He is both a visionary and an entertainer; he is interested, as he continually says he is, in extending our knowledge of and power of control over human conduct and emotion, but, at the same time, he is always conscious of the entertainment value of what he says, saying it as he does brilliantly. Conversely, although he is an entertainer, he does not at all abandon the self-regard of those who have a "vision," even though it be for him a borrowed one; instead, he will display the particular vision he has at the moment with conscious and virtuoso skill. One of the most logical themes for such a poet would be to combine these two sides of his poetic personality and to teach us knowledge of and control over all those parts of the mind and the heart that are responsive to skill with language, to entertainment, and, most generally, to everything aesthetic; indeed, this is the major theme of Auden's most self-conscious poetry.

[22] "John Skelton," *The Great Tudors*, ed. Katherine Garvin (London: I. Nicholson and Watson, 1935), p. 67.

5. Idea and Voice

With the poems in *Look, Stranger!* Auden enters fully into the synthesis of thought so familiar to critics as the structural and intellectual backbone of his thirties' poetry; the aggressive nonsense of the earliest work yields for the most part to a more serious use of the ideas of Freud and Marx. The role of these ideas in his poetry has always been a central preoccupation of early critics of Auden but has been confined primarily to the explication of where these ideas appear in the poems, in a nearly impossible attempt to determine just when Auden was this and when that. Such investigations are of course important. With Auden, however, they can be, if pursued with too zealous a literalness, misleading, for they tend to obscure a matter of far greater importance: what these ideas mean to Auden both as a person and as a poet.

When one wonders what Auden felt about the ideas he used, one is confronted with a number of striking facts that want explanation. Most odd is the gap between Auden's sensibility and the sensibilities of the thinkers by whom he has been most deeply influenced; to examine the nature and significance of this gap is to illuminate certain aspects of Auden's sensibility not normally examined by critics but

158

rather seen as discrediting defects. One need only note a few of the obvious and overwhelming characteristics of the life and work of Marx and Freud to become aware of the differences between them and Auden. Both Marx and Freud were profoundly individualistic and original thinkers; with Freud, this originality had the curious side effect of making him often completely unreceptive to ideas he could not fit into his own particular frame of thought, so that, if one did not accept him as teacher, one had difficulty communicating with him. A corollary to this is that both Freud and Marx were systematic thinkers; they not only brought diverse data of experience into a comprehensive order, but also attempted to explain all experience in terms of their systems and spent their lives altering, expanding, and adapting these systems to new ends. Moreover, with Freud and Marx, system is simultaneously dogma, and the fact that their thought was meant to be applied to reality, to be put into effect, made its rigorous elaboration all the more an absolute necessity.

The contrast of such traits to what we know of Auden's sensibility is glaring. Where Freud was incapable of absorbing foreign ideas, Auden is a virtuoso of intellectual receptivity; his freedom of mind depends upon his ability to make connections between ideas in widely different realms with exuberant and spontaneous ease. Where Freud and Marx were independent and original thinkers, Auden is a marvelously adaptive spirit, able not just to be influenced by those whom he has copiously read, but also to pick up ideas nimbly, on a very fleeting acquaintance; in addition, there is an element of fashionable dilletantism present in Auden's interests, which one sees both in the fact that, in the thirties, Freud and Marx were the avant-garde rage and in the fact that Auden tends to develop his ideas in the context of small groups of like-minded thinkers. Finally, although Auden has always been primarily attracted to systematic philosophers, his own use of ideas is not strict or systematic; what is most confusing to those who try to pin down the essential Auden is the fact that he overuses these ideas, that is, he uses them in too many different and often contradictory ways; one simply cannot select any one of his formulations as central and seminal.

In terms of personality as well Auden differs radically from Freud and Marx; his freedom of spirit, his irreverence, and his hedonistic self-indulgence actually clash with the asceticism, the overwhelming earnestness and dedication to rational coherence and scientific exactitude of Freud and Marx. Whereas Freud and Marx are thinkers trying to make their ideas as responsibly faithful to reality as possible, Auden is a man whose energy is never fully bound by the content of any of his ideas. In this connection, one of Freud's descriptions of the role of nonsense in the emotional life of the child has an interesting relevance:

> And he [the child] puts words together without regard to the condition that they should make sense, in order to obtain from them the pleasurable effect of rhythm and rhyme. Little by little he is forbidden this enjoyment, until all that remains permitted to him are significant combinations of words. But when he is older attempts still emerge at disregarding the restrictions that have been learnt on the use of words. Words are disfigured by particular little additions being made to them, their forms are altered by certain manipulations,

. . . or a private language may be constructed for use among playmates. These attempts are found again and again among certain categories of mental patients.

Whatever the motive may have been which led the child to begin these games, I believe that in his later development he gives himself up to them with the consciousness that they are nonsensical, and that he finds enjoyment in the attraction of what is forbidden by reason. He now uses games in order to withdraw from the pressure of critical reason. But there is far more potency in the restrictions which must establish themselves in the course of a child's education in logical thinking and in distinguishing between what is true and false in reality; and for this reason the rebellion against the compulsion of logic and reality is deepgoing and long-lasting. Even the phenomena of imaginative activity must be included in this [rebellious] category, the power of criticism has increased so greatly in the later part of childhood and in the period of learning which extends over puberty that the pleasure in 'liberated nonsense' only seldom dares to show itself directly. One does not venture to be absurd.[1]

This statement is applicable to Auden in a surprisingly large number of ways. For example, the description of the nonsense in the psychology of the child corresponds closely to the nature, tone, and material of the "childish" Mortmere fantasies. The Mortmere group did have a private

---

[1] Sigmund Freud, *Jokes and Their Relation to the Unconscious*, in *The Standard Edition of the Complete Psychological Works of Sigmund Freud*, ed. James Strachey (London: The Hogarth Press, 1960), VIII, 126–127.

language; it represented an indulgence in and use of infantile modes of behavior and expression; it was based on pleasure in nonsense; and it was rebellious in this use of nonsense. Certain of these Mortmere traits endure, in analagous forms, into Auden's later work; the hint of a private language remains behind the common analytic language of the thirties, and the trait Freud ascribes to nonsense, the primacy of the "pleasurable effect of rhythm and rhyme" over sense, corresponds to our impression that throughout Auden's work poetic form is a consideration prior to sense and often functions heuristically in the creation of a poem. But what makes Freud's description especially interesting for a study of Auden is the final disparity between the assumptions behind the statement and our understanding of Auden's character. To put it simply, with Auden, the Freudian dialectic of education does not work; although Auden does "grow out" of an early indulgence in nonsense, this growth is not marked by the psychological struggle of a pleasure-seeking *Ich* struggling to evade an iron reality but finally more or less bound by it in the bands of logic and the awesome distinction between true and not-true. From what we know of Auden's education this is biographically not the case. Auden was a university prankster, and one could try to relate this fact to Freud's comment that the child's rebellious and nonsensical pursuit of pleasure reasserts itself in the student's *Bierschwefel,* a state of soul characterized by the line in *Faust,* "Mit wenig Witz and viel Behagen" ("With little wit and much pleasure"); to make this connection, however, would be wrong.[2] Auden's early fantasies

[2] Ibid., p. 126.

can hardly be equated with the muddy dullness and banal revelry of a *Bierschwefel* and are better described as activities pursued "Mit viel Witz und viel Behagen." The crucial difference is that education for Auden was not a repressive disciplining of energies directed toward pleasure but rather something that aided him in his pursuit of pleasure through the exercise of wit; Spender's description of Auden at Oxford is of a person who took advantage of the years of relative leisure to "fulfill his potentialities, obtain satisfaction for his desires, and maintain his attitudes, without prejudice and without accepting any authority outside his own judgement."[3]

Similarly, in Auden's work one is unable to find any trace of a subjection of fantasy to reality by means of "logical thinking" and serious use of the distinction between "what is true and false in reality"; Auden makes continual use of this distinction, for one of the staples of his poetic rhetoric is to show how an attitude, emotion, or idea is in reality false, but this is a staple of *poetic* rhetoric, something dedicated to intellectual pleasure, and as such something far different from "distinguishing between the true and false *in reality*." The sense we have of Auden during the thirties is that he lived in a quirky, willful suspension of the true and false, that for him all experience was humorously interpreted as fictional; one side of his characteristic self-parody in seeming earnestness is to reveal all his experience as partly make-believe, and his role as an "Uncle Wiz" is one of a self-made figure of myth humorously conscious of his own unreality as such.

[3] Spender, *World within World* (London: Hamish Hamilton, 1951), p. 53.

There are a number of ways to define Auden's peculiar suspension of the "laws" of reality. One has the sense that Auden's energy is never fully bound by the content of his ideas; there is always the feeling of a Dadaistic *Nichts* behind Auden's "beliefs," for they seem to be held as if they were "answers" to life; there is always the feeling that Auden's poetic formulations are provisional to the poem he is then writing and thus played with rather than believed; and one feels that Auden is more interested in the ritual of believing than in the belief itself. To these observations we can add still others, that Auden's assertions are generally derivative from other thinkers, that they are being used experimentally (an observation also relevant to Auden's use of poetic form, even when it is an eminently traditional one, such as the sonnet or the verse essay), that the ideas are used too often and in too many different contexts to cohere finally into a body of thought, and that Auden's changes of belief are to be explained not only as changes of heart but also as exhaustion of or boredom with the ideas. Behind all of these attempts to grasp what seems most elusive in Auden, his attitude toward the ideas he asserts, lies one basic and oddly simple axiom: Auden is always conscious of his ideas as a part of literary expression, and, as such, he sees their primary end to be pleasure rather than truth. If a poet like Auden, then, does have genuine beliefs, their authenticity will be based on something wholly outside the realm of verbal expression; to be sure, faith and poetry may overlap at certain points, but, in essence, the two realms are always distinct from one another.[4] That this

[4] One of Auden's attempts to define the areas of overlap should be quoted here; in an essay, "Writing," in *The Dyer's Hand* (New

conviction has considerable importance for Auden's practice as a poet will become clear later; here, it will be sufficient to note that it is implicit in Auden's habit of making use of extrapoetic dogmas for his poetry, be they from psychoanalysis, politics, or theology, and that it raises a unique aesthetic problem for Auden's poetry. The success of one of Auden's poems depends not only on how well he uses the ideas he has chosen for it; it also depends on how skillfully, tactfully, and justly he manages to incorporate the sense that he is pointing beyond the poem to some ulterior truth. In essence, one could argue that the problem is unsolvable, something that is supported by readers' frequent impatience with Auden's "schoolmasterly tone." If that which is pointed to is embedded too fully in the poem, then its authority as an extrapoetic truth is vitiated; if it is simply pointed to, then it is poetically unconvincing. Or, to put it another way: how can a poem establish something as an important truth, when its validity, by definition, is not within the province of the poem and may even be un-

York: Random House, 1948), p. 19, he makes the following comment about poetry and belief: "What makes it difficult for a poet not to tell lies is that, in poetry, all facts and all beliefs cease to be true or false and become interesting possibilities. The reader does not have to share the beliefs expressed in a poem in order to enjoy it. Knowing this, a poet is constantly tempted to make use of an idea of a belief, not because he believes it to be true, but because he sees that it has interesting poetic possibilities. It may not, perhaps, be absolutely necessary that he *believe* it, but it is certainly necessary that his emotions be deeply involved, and this they can never be unless, as a man, he takes it more seriously than as a mere poetic contrivance." Reprinted by permission of Random House, copyright 1948, 1950, 1952, 1953, 1954; © 1956, 1957, 1958, 1960, 1962, by W. H. Auden.

dermined when exposed to poetic treatment? Even if this problem remains unsolvable, it indicates what is perhaps the most sophisticated way to consider Auden's success in individual poems and development as a poet; rather than concentrating solely on the changes in his ideas or the fact that his poems become progressively richer in number and variety of ideas, we should examine how effectively he manages to bridge the gap between an avowedly fictional voice and the various truths he so persistently seeks to refer to. From this standpoint, much of his political writing during the thirties is dissatisfying; too often Auden's parodic voice and reliance on fantasy, by means of which he tries simultaneously to exhibit the inventiveness of fiction and to assert the truth of dogma, results in a confusion or lack of control of tone rather than a bridging of the gap between word and belief.

Given, then, the extent of the gap between Auden and his sources of the thirties, Marx and Freud, we are impelled to ask a second question: just why should Auden have been attracted to these particular thinkers, who are in many ways so alien to his personality and to each other? The answer to this question is not simply that Auden, as a mobile *Zeitgeist*, was in the forefront of the fashion of his time, although this fact is indeed quite important. There is also some pattern behind Auden's preoccupation with such unlike types, something we have encountered before in a different context. The synthesis of Marx and Freud forms a structure of thought which, when viewed with an eye to its possibilities, generates a large number of poetic ideas; Freud and Marx juxtaposed are as suggestive of poetic material as was the juxtaposition of disparate sources in *Paid on Both Sides* and "Journal of an Airman." What Auden has done is to pick two systems of thought that are widely divergent but comparable and complementary in a number of interesting ways. Both Freud and Marx serve to undermine the liberal tradition, and both unmask conventional notions of reality in order to reveal the real necessity behind them; and this dialectic is the rationale for most of Auden's early rhetoric. In addition, they are admirable complementaries, for they have staked out disparate but related territories for thought: Freud deals with the individual mind and Marx with social forces; Freud is concerned with inner necessity while Marx is a student of historical law. That Freud's perspective is in many ways antagonistic to that of Marx is not damaging; it becomes a positive good, for Auden can exercise his ingenuity in working out two such perspectives simultaneously and, in doing so, have the satisfaction of reconciling two apparently opposed philosophies, each of which claims to present a comprehensive explanation of reality. In thus reconciling dogmas, Auden would achieve what is, in a certain sense, a full picture of the world; it is a full picture that is achieved by ingeniously fitting two halves together.

That Auden's mind is stimulated by this process of "working out" the disparate systems is not evidenced by his poems alone; numerous examples of it occur in the essays, examples that reveal the ingenuity of Auden's mind more baldly than the poems. The clearest summary and contrast of psychology and communism occurs in Auden's essay "The Good Life":

> Psychology and Communism have certain points in common:

(1) They are both concerned with unmasking hidden conflicts.

(2) Both regard these conflicts as inevitable stages which must be made to negate themselves.

(3) Both regard thought and knowledge not as something spontaneous and self-sufficient, but as purposive and determined by the conflict between instinctive needs and a limited environment. Communism stresses hunger and the larger social mass affected by it; psychology, love and the small family unit. (Biological nutrition is anterior to reproduction, so that the Communist approach would seem from this standpoint the more basic one.) . . .

(4) Both desire and believe in the possibility of freedom of action and choice, which can only be obtained by unmasking and making conscious the hidden conflict.

The hostility of Communism to psychology is that it accuses the latter of failing to draw correct conclusions from its data. Finding the neurotic a product of society, it attempts to adjust him to that society, i. e. it ignores the fact that the neurotic has a real grievance.[5]

What Auden has done is to put one system of ideas up against another and note the similarities and antagonisms; this rather mechanical process is carried out even more methodically at another place in the essay, where Auden makes a list (a,b,x,y) of possible answers to a question posed of communism, social democracy, Christianity, and psy-

[5] *Christianity and the Social Revolution,* ed. J. Lewis, K. Polanyi, and D. Kitchin (New York: Scribner, 1936), pp. 46–47.

chology, and then answers that question for each item by listing after it the relevant symbols.

To call this habit of mind simply mechanical is of course not enough; it is indeed that, but it is also related to a variety of more significant characteristics of Auden's way of thought. Such a cast of mind, especially when seen in its more complex forms, is a mark of one who enjoys playing with structures of thought for their own sakes. For example, in his book reviews, Auden enjoys creating instant frameworks of thought, be they of literary history or of structural analysis, within which the book in question may be placed; in *The Enchafed Flood*, on the other hand, Auden generates a theory of romanticism from a limited number of works of writers of different orders of seriousness and different backgrounds (Wordsworth, Melville, Baudelaire, Ibsen, Valéry, and Lewis Carroll), and the resulting theory, though capricious and unsatisfying as literary scholarship, is a source of more exciting individual ideas than many of the products of systematic scholarship. In such a poem as "Out on the lawn I lie in bed" one sees a similar process at work; a union of Freud and Marx provides a structure of ideas generative of some very beautiful and seemingly quite personal poetic language. That Auden is stimulated by playing with structures of thought, and turns especially to systematic thinkers for his ideas, is related to other predispositions; Auden's imposition of strictures on what could go into his fantasy landscape of mines and decayed industry aided him in the construction of a childhood fantasy world, and he has been consistently drawn to playing with predetermined literary forms.

A person who enjoys playing with structures of thought

may have much in common with certain very recognizable types, types to which Auden has often been compared. First, there is much of the schoolboy and the scholar in someone whose ideas are generated by outside material with which he concerns himself. Both the impulse to work the material out into a lively order and the provisionality of that order to the purpose at hand are characteristic of the intellectual student, in whom the schoolboy asserts himself in an impulse toward irresponsibility and latent parody of thought and in whom the scholar is evident in the more serious ingenuity of the impulse to capture and explain as much material as possible by means of intellectual constructs. At the same time, when a variety of ideas is carried lightly, with a certain elegance, with the knowledge of the traditions behind these ideas, and with a cultivated pleasure at being able to draw so readily upon these ideas for entertaining discourse, we encounter the type of the sophisticated man; for this man, expression is peculiarly derivative from language, both from his pleasure in his command of language and literary form and from what he has encountered in the form of language, that is, all that he has read and absorbed.[6]

It is time now to turn directly to the word that has been used over and over again in this book to describe the spirit behind Auden's verse—the word "play"; we can no longer use this word without some attempt to explain exactly how

[6] R. Roth's essay, "The Sophistication of W. H. Auden: A Sketch in Longinian Method," *Modern Philolgy*, 48 (1951), 193–204, illustrates well Auden's sophistication as a writer of elegies. Roth's attempt to see in Auden a sublime poet is less commendable.

it applies to Auden. In Auden's commonplace book, *A Certain World*, he notes the famous assertion made by Friedrich Schiller in his *On the Aesthetic Education of Man:* "Man only plays when, in the full meaning of the word, he is a man, and he is only completely a man when he plays." This sense of play is certainly applicable to the civilized humanism of much of Auden's verse; nevertheless, we must make distinctions between what Schiller meant by the word "play" and what we mean in applying it to Auden. Schiller's statement about play is meant to be ultimately "capable of bearing the whole edifice of the art of the beautiful, and of the still more difficult art of living."[7] We are concerned with understanding play only insofar as it helps us to speak of a particular kind of verse. One clue that shows us how we must limit our understanding of "play" is provided by the advice given to Schiller (which he did not take) to avoid the use of the word "*spielen*" (to play) because of "*unedle Nebenideen*" ("ignoble connotations"), that is, its connection with such activities as *Skatspielen* ("playing Skat," the card game); Schiller kept the word because he did not want to sever all connection between ordinary language and activities and a theory of art finally oriented toward the sublime.[8] With Auden, however, it is exactly the ordinary meaning of "play" that is crucial to defining his kind of art. Auden is a player, a gamesman, for whom art is the most difficult, various, and interesting of games, to be played at its best with a masterful skill, and a

[7] Schiller, *On the Aesthetic Education of Man*, trans. E. M. Wilkinson and L. A. Willoughby (Oxford: Clarendon Press, 1967), pp. 107–109.

[8] Ibid., pp. 331–332.

successful poem is characterized by all the delight and vividness of a game in which all of one's faculties are provisionally engaged, that is, engaged for the purpose of that game.

Auden's gamesmanship is readily apparent in the distinctive surface of his verse. His characteristic reliance on material that has already been, in one way or another, previously stylized is essential to his poetic game-playing; he does not need to create so much as play with his material, to find ways of enlivening it by the motion and surprise of his verse, by the facility with which it is handled and the novel justice of the contexts found for it. We have discussed the way in which Auden creatively draws his ideas from outside sources; that the same is true of much of his rhetoric and of his poetic form, a short look at the sonnets in his and Isherwood's *Journey to a War* will show. For the ideas, form, and rhetoric of the sonnets, Rilke is the principal model; he uses Rilke's development of the sonnet in a way that ranges from parody to emulation, but which almost always carries with it the air of an experiment or tour de force. Most obvious is that he has absorbed with ease much of the Rilkean verbal apparatus; one is continually reminded of the *Sonnets to Orpheus* in Auden's use of characteristic imagery, of indefinite pronouns, of a poetic fable allegorically suggestive of a philosophical point, of an abrupt beginning, of the narrative conjunction "and," and of tropes based on conceiving "the human life in terms of landscape."[9] More deeply, Auden has borrowed a number

[9] Auden, "Rilke in English," *The New Republic*, 100 (Sept. 6, 1939), 135. Some of the list of Auden's borrowings is taken from

of ideas from Rilke as well, as in, for example, Sonnet I, Auden is concerned to define the nature of Man's self-consciousness, and, like Rilke, he does it by playing man off against the animals, in certain ways to the detriment of man. The conclusion is close to Rilke's argument in the first Elegy: "dass wir nicht sehr verlässlich zu Haus sind / in der gedeuteten Welt" ("that we are not very reliably at home / in the interpreted world").[10]

Sonnet I, although derivative from Rilke in both ideas and rhetoric, gives us at the same time certain indications of how Auden is changing Rilke's ideas and rhetoric by adapting them to a different purpose; the line "Fish swam as fish, peach settled into peach"[11] is a shorthand summary of Rilke's fixation with understanding and presenting *Dinge* (flowers, fruit, stone, etc.) through what Geoffrey Hartman calls "les yeux du corps," that is, through a transcendental vision of them in their physical nature.[12] The action of peach settling into peach-being is, however, so quick and witty a summary of Rilke that it very nearly constitutes a parody; this closeness to parody is accented even further by the line "The hour of birth their only time at college," a line which deflates anything that might be left

Monroe Spears, *The Poetry of W. H. Auden* (New York: Oxford University Press), p. 149.

[10] R. M. Rilke, *Gesammelte Gedichte* (Frankfurt on the Main: Insel-Verlag, 1962), p. 441.

[11] *Journey to a War* (New York: Random House, 1939), p. 259. Selections from *Journey to a War* reprinted by permission of Faber and Faber, Ltd., and Random House, Inc.; copyright, 1939, by W. H. Auden and Christopher Isherwood.

[12] *The Unmediated Vision* (New York: Harcourt, Brace and World, 1966), p. 95.

of Rilke's elegiac mysticism. This deflation is finally not simply parody; what Auden is attempting at the same time is a serious reworking of Rilke in a new context, that of poetry relating to a report on wartime China, poetry which, although definitely philosophical verse in its abstraction and its concern with ideas, has one foot planted solidly in political journalism. By now we should no longer be surprised that Auden has chosen Rilke as a model; the very inappropriateness of the Rilkean sonnet to journalistic experience would have caught Auden's fancy.[13]

The sonnet that provides the best example of how Rilke was reworked into poetry about China is Sonnet XIII; it begins with a Rilkean imperative and a number of Rilkean images:

> Certainly praise: let the song mount again and again
> For life as it blossoms out in a jar or a face,
> For the vegetable patience, the animal grace;
> Some people have been happy; there have been great
>   men.[14]

Once again, a line like "the vegetable patience, the animal grace" puts any notion of *rühmen* (to praise) in a Rilkean sense quite out of joint; such wit is finally antagonistic to song. With the second stanza, however, the basis for Auden's debate with Rilke reveals itself:

[13] There would have been other reasons as well; in his essays, Auden reveals that he took Rilke, in ways to be discussed below, as a kind of model for poets in wartime. Also, the encounter with Rilke at this time was probably dependent largely on circumstance, in that Auden had probably taken a copy of Rilke to China with him just as he had taken *Don Juan* to Iceland.

[14] *Journey to a War*, p. 271.

> But hear the morning's injured weeping, and know
>   why:
> Cities and men have fallen; the will of the Unjust
> Has never lost its power; still, all princes must
> Employ the Fairly-Noble unifying Lie.

The poem thus takes on Rilke directly; against Rilke's "Rühmen, das ists!"[15] is directed the qualified command "Certainly praise," and Rilke's attempt to absorb experience into song, to maintain that *"Gesang ist Dasein"*[16] ("song is existence") is countered by Auden's consciousness of a history that "opposes its grief to our buoyant song," his attempt to heighten and focus our awareness of history's daily events rather than to transcend them.

Unlike Rilke, Auden is not concerned with creating a poetic myth or image as a part of a mystic quest, the attempt to reach the "unheard center";[17] nor is Auden's process of composition something genuinely contemplative, a process in which ideas and images emerge simultaneously from intuition and reason. Almost all of the sonnets should be interpreted as play about a certain, wittily didactic point, and the play must be seen as play within a number of "givens," that is within a body of rhetoric, ideas, and images derived in the main from outside sources, ranging from popular stereotypes to literary history but in particular the work of one poet, and which would lie as if preformed in the vocabulary of the wittily intelligent. As an

15 Rilke, p. 491.
16 Ibid., 488.
17 Another term from Hartman, who took it in turn from Rilke, p. 94.

illustration of these comments an analysis of Sonnet **XXVII** will be helpful; it is in this poem that Auden most clearly reveals his philosophical argument, a humanist analysis of the nature of man's freedom, an analysis related on the one hand to the Marxist humanism of "Spain" and on the other hand to the existential imperative that man must become conscious of his absolute responsibility for himself. The poem puts its argument—its particular "point"—in a single line: "We live in freedom by necessity."[18] That this idea is in a sense derivative is clear; Auden has wittily transformed Engels' famous dictum that "freedom is the consciousness of necessity" into a statement that no longer concerns the relation of the individual consciousness to historical law but rather the aloneness and fallibility of man within a world that gives him no assurances.

The poem's structural movement is a gradual focusing in upon this point by means of suggesting the alternatives to it, the various wishful escapes we would gladly make from the knowledge of our condition; the images for these escapes are themselves witty summations of ideas that are taken from and refer to a variety of outside sources rather than to specific experience. Most simply, one notes several images probably taken from Rilke, such as the "taste of joy in the innocent mouth" and the fountains' perfection (an image which could as well have come from Yeats, in whom Auden was also interested at this time); and the poem's controlling image—that we are "Wandering lost upon the mountains of our choice"—is Auden borrowing from himself, for it is the familiar Auden tops of mountains

[18] *Journey to a War*, p. 285.

as symbols for conditions or actions of the psyche.[19] A
more interesting case of Auden's use of outside sources is
the reference to the "ancient South, / . . . the warm nude
ages of instinctive poise." Here our knowledge of sources
for the lines becomes more actively a part of the pleasure
of the poem, for the lines' delightful wit can only be explained by the way they play upon, summarize, and put
ideas already familiar to us from literature, the way the
lines suggest a Germanic yearning for the South of beautiful forms, a nostalgia for the Golden Age, and a Rousseau-
istic desire for a primitivist idyll. Similarly, the idea of
dreaming "of a part / In the glorious balls of the future"
plays humorously upon the familiar fairy-tale situation of
an impoverished heroine dreaming of the ball at which she
will meet the handsome prince as well as upon the time-
honored image of the dance as a symbol for social concord,
and the poem's most complex image, that of the "intricate
maze," is familiar to us as a form of the often-used and,
after Kafka, modish idea of life as a labyrinth; Auden's
handling of this image is especially pleasing in the way it
gracefully and easily understands and resolves all the implications of the labyrinth. The maze's confusion is re-
placed by "a plan"; this plan is not just an intellectual solution, dry and passionless, but rather something that is
accessible to instinct and reason working together, in the
form of a "disciplined" heart. The result is that the labyrinth is transformed into something that suggests another
traditional image; a place in which the heart "Can follow
for ever and ever its harmless ways" would be very like a

[19] Another use of this topos quite close to its use in Sonnet
XXVII is found in Poem XX of *Look, Stranger!*.

garden, in which easeful innocence may roam the many shady paths in pleasure and contentment. To describe this image as the labyrinth turned garden as a result of a unification of heart and mind, impulse and discipline, sounds of course bloodlessly abstract; there is more than a touch of this abstraction in the lines themselves, for Auden is a poet not only aware of these images as literary archetypes but also engaged in just this kind of speculation. In Auden's poem, however, what would otherwise be bloodless abstraction is enlivened by its grace of expression, the way it is borne by its imagery and the way it is fitted without strain or clumsiness into the sonnet's artificial little room.

The principal effect of Auden's reworking of already stylized forms, rhetoric, and ideas has been described by John Bayley, in what is the most sympathetic and accurate analysis to date of the tone of Auden's verse; by means of using language that calls attention to its own stylization and then arranging this language in a poetic argument that flows with an alacrity and verve so great that it appears conscious of its own virtuosity, Auden exhibits to us his delight in "turning into poetry—in 'nullifying' into the poetic as Sartre might call it—the most ragged and 'viscous' aspects and experiences of life."[20] Thus, in the very texture of Auden's verse, the chief quality of a gamesman is evident: the assertion, either covert or overt, that what one is doing is a game, a conscious unreality in which one's skill and mastery are displayed and at the same time qualified, in that one retains always the brisk, self-deprecatory consciousness that one is engaging in a self-enclosed, gra-

---

[20] *The Romantic Survival* (London: Constable, 1960), p. 151.

tuitous activity which finally has no relevance to anything outside itself. Thus, we return to and find ourselves able to restate the problem raised earlier in this chapter: how can a poet with this sort of sensibility successfully attempt to deal with material that claims to transcend the game of poetry? Or, even more fundamentally, how can such a sensibility even deal with itself, with its own self-containment and self-deprecation? Since Auden's most remarkable attempts to make poetry point beyond itself occur after he has abandoned his political orientation of the thirties, a discussion of the former question will be postponed until the next chapter; here, we will restrict ourselves to a consideration of the latter problem.

Auden's gamesmanship considered in the abstract can be more than a little chilling. With its constant awareness of language and expression generally as a primarily fictional mode, it undercuts all naive belief in the efficacy of expression and tends ultimately toward an artistic solipsism, which, paradoxically, asserts itself more convincingly as solipsistic the more fully it avails itself of the means of expression, of gesture, word, idea, image, and symbol. The result would seem to be an isolation of oneself from all human intercourse in the midst of cultural richness; reality would not be kept intact on the margins of the game, but would rather be banished to a realm outside all that one could ever articulate. One would be left with a kind of modern agony: a sense of vacancy that one cannot name or expiate by naming, because it is itself the hollowness that resides at the heart of all expression. A brute howl might seem to be the answer, but, then, that too has been stylized by the Expressionists and one could never remove this knowledge from his mind, even in mid-howl; similarly, silence as a form of literary despair has already received a great deal of critical notice. It would seem then that the gamesman would have no other recourse than to sit isolated amid his own conscious scrutiny and force himself to keep at the old game of dazzle, a game whose ultimate achievement is its own self-deprecation.

Such despair is never to be seen in Auden's work, and one can perhaps do no more than say that the reasons for Auden's avoidance of it are, in a profound sense, constitutional. Auden's sheer gusto for poetic virtuosity is the chief constitutional element of his verse; similarly constitutional is the fact that he never pauses in his energetic experimentation with the resources of language and idea, even though the fruits of such experimentation are shown to be only games. The energy involved seems to stem from an ever-unchecked childish *Spieltrieb* (play-drive); it may be also seen as an indication of an innate, ineradicable optimism and feeling of spiritual health. But most important to Auden's poetry—and certainly to his poetry of the thirties—is that, although his poetic activity tends toward an ultimately solipsistic ideal, he has never lost faith in it as having a kind of social importance. This does not mean the social importance of "relevant" writing, the literature of *engagement;* instead, it refers to the importance of literature that plays upon and expresses the values and ideas of a community of readers and that thus helps to bring together and keep intact that community. Auden, throughout the thirties, distinguished himself by the fact that he never lost social reference in a society that believed itself to have fallen apart. His career was one of expanding social reference: from the Mortmere group to the group theater to a public that transcends the dialectic of radical politics. More important, he has managed to use, more extensively than any other modern poet, the inheritance of a seemingly disrupted tradition; one indication of this is that he is one of the very few poets in the twentieth century who has managed to perceive and capture contemporary manners. That he should be able to perceive possibilities of social reference in an age when social forms have been seriously disrupted or even wholly undercut is also perhaps a constitutional virtue; as we have seen, it is paradoxically the very disruption of social forms that has liberated his artistic reference to them. During the thirties, he thrived especially as a member of groups which, in some way or another, called attention to themselves as being as much mythical as they were real;[21] conversely, one of the chief preoccupations of his poetry has been the construction of myths of societies that might perhaps some day become real, be they visions of a Marxist Utopia or of a more patently fictional "Just Society" and "Good Place."

[21] Even Auden's solitude has expressed itself in characteristic mixtures of the real and the mythical. As a child, he contrived elaborate fantasies of landscapes of mines and industry; at the same time, this landscape could not include any implement which was not real. Similarly, in later life, Auden greeted the fact of advanced age in a distinctive manner; he suddenly decided that he was an old man and began to perform, both fancifully and seriously, all the rituals of his new role.

6. After the Thirties

In *Another Time*, Auden continued a poetic development first evident in the sonnets and the "Commentary" in *Journey to a War:* an increased ease in writing a fully public, cultivated verse and a dramatic widening of intellectual and literary interests. A new, freer use of ideas emerged in the play with poetic summaries of historical movements in "Commentary," "September 1, 1939," and "Epithalameon," and the work of a variety of writers is expressed in more complexity than merely their inclusion in the Marxist or neo-Mortmerian drama of conflict between an ally and an enemy; writers and their ideas are fictionalized, dramatized, and appraised in a series of specifically literary poems, including both the famous elegies on Yeats, Freud, and Toller and the poems on Voltaire, Pascal, Rimbaud, and Melville. Accompanying this change is a gradual reappraisal which is a coda to Auden's political interest of the thirties and prelude to the "middle phase," in which, to the disillusionment of many of his admirers, he distanced himself from left-wing politics.

This transitional period was marked by experiment with a political attitude derivative principally from Rilke and Yeats; Auden was attempting to formulate a way in which a poet's voice could be of compelling political relevance without being subservient to any particular program for action. A review of Rilke's poetry gives an indication of Auden's thought:

> But Rilke's influence is not confined to certain technical tricks. It is, I believe, no accident that as the international crisis becomes more and more acute, the poet to whom writers are becoming increasingly drawn should be one who felt that it was pride and presumption to interfere with the lives of others (for each is unique and the apparent misfortunes of each may be his very way of salvation); one who occupied himself consistently and exclusively with his own inner life; one who wrote
>
> 'Art cannot be helpful through our trying to keep and specially concerning ourselves with the distresses of others, but in so far as we bear our own distresses more passionately, give now and then a perhaps clearer meaning to endurance, and develop for ourselves the means of expressing the suffering within us and its conquest more precisely and clearly than is possible to those who have to apply their powers to something else.'
>
> This tendency is not to be dismissed with the cheery cry "defeatism." It implies not a denial of the impulse to political action, but rather the realization that if the writer is not to harm both others and himself, he must consider, and very much more humbly and patiently than he has been doing, what kind of person he is, and what may be his real function. When the ship catches

fire, it seems only natural to rush importantly to the pumps, but perhaps one is only adding to the general confusion and panic: to sit still and pray seems selfish and unheroic, but it may be the wisest and most helpful course.[1]

The parody of those who "rush importantly to the pumps" is both a form of sniping at the political enthusiasms of the thirties and a recognition of the fact that the peculiar stability in the midst of political tumult, a major quality of the Baldwin Era in England, has broken down; the time is now one of a crisis of more threatening order, a time when international war is in the offing, war that can no longer be isolated and idealized as were the early stages of the conflict in Spain.

In the elegy on Yeats Auden argues that

> . . . poetry makes nothing happen: it survives
> In the valley of its saying where executives
> Would never want to tamper. . . .[2]

Instead, what poetry can do is

> Still persuade us to rejoice;
>
> With the farming of a verse
> Make a vineyard of the curse,

[1] Auden, "Rilke in English," *The New Republic*, 100 (1939), 135.

[2] *The Collected Poetry of W. H. Auden* (New York: Random House, 1945), p. 50. Selections reprinted by permission of Faber and Faber, Ltd., and Random House, Inc.; copyright, 1945, by W. H. Auden.

Sing of human unsuccess
In a rapture of distress;

In the deserts of the heart
Let the healing fountain start,
In the prison of his days
Teach the free man how to praise.

Both opinions stem from Auden's thought about Yeats; the former opinion is formed in argument with Yeats and the latter is a remark that makes a hopeful gloss on the Yeatsian phenomenon of the poetic curse, suggesting that mere distress can become at least "a rapture of distress" when put into poetry. Auden's imitative and interpretive ability is crucial to the success of his poems on writers; the imitation corresponds as well to Auden's own peculiarly literary shopping about for a new political stance, and this becomes clear in "September 1, 1939" in the way Auden makes use of Yeats, both of his bitter audacity of reference, his calling on the famous dead in a tone both cavalier and off-hand yet urgently intense, and of his rhetoric of affirmation from the bottomless abyss of a poetic curse. Like "Spain, 1937," this is an occasional poem related to a historical situation (September 1 was the date of the fascist invasion of Poland); now, however, the "today" is not the time of the struggle but rather a time of a hateful, vicious, distorted, and hopeless normality, and the just are no longer united and capable of meaningful political action.[3]

[3] The various references of "September 1, 1939" are all easily explained. Light is shed on the connection of Luther to the present crisis by Auden's review "Jacob and the Angel," *The New Republic*, 101 (1939), 292–293, and the reference to Linz, a reference to the *Anschluss*, is explained by Phyllis Bartlett and John

The *New Year Letter* is the first major statement of Auden's re-evaluation of politics (or, in other terms, recantation of his old commitment). He speaks directly to the question in the second part of the poem:

> We hoped; we waited for the day
> The state would wither clean away,
> Expecting the Millenium
> The theory promised us would come,
> It didn't. Specialists must try
> To detail all the reasons why;
> Meanwhile at least the layman knows
> That none are lost so soon as those
> Who overlook their crooked nose.[4]

Shortly thereafter, in *For the Time Being*, the tombstone is dropped over the recent grave by the admission of Herod, who, although a liberal and thus a figure of parody to Auden in his thirties phase, now stands for the political man in general: "I object. I'm a liberal. I want everyone to be happy. I wish I had never been born."[5] The change is fast and a complete about-face; the reader is left asking what happened.

Biographically, several things did happen. First, Auden

Pollard in *The Explicator*, 14 (1955), Item 8. Auden's use of Thucydides is based on Pericles' funeral oration (*The Peloponnesian War*, II, 35; see also *New Year Letter*, notes to line 720) in that the democratic ideal espoused therein contrasts so glaringly with Athenian practice. The comment by Nijinsky may be found in *The Diary of Vaslav Nijinsky* (London: Jonathan Cape, 1966), p. 25.

[4] *The Collected Poetry*, p. 288.

[5] Ibid., p. 460.

emigrated to America, self-consciously choosing the role of the literary exile and leaving behind a disgruntled English literary group. That breaking off old literary ties was a principal reason for Auden's move is indicated by a comment of Cyril Connolly: "He reverts always to the same argument, that a writer needs complete anonymity, he must break away from the European literary happy family."[6]

To leave this family behind and to educate himself in the anonymity of New York City shows considerable courage and self-awareness on the part of the poet in Auden; although he was cutting himself loose from a major source of his popularity and previous creativity, he was doing what was necessary for his poetic growth, not only in disassociating himself from the moribund movement of the thirties in England, but also in schooling himself in a new privacy from which he could reevaluate both man's relation to society and man's relation to God.

Second, Auden experienced a religious conversion; this gave him an intellectual position from which to reevaluate his former "beliefs." Instead of renouncing all he had experienced and thought, Auden had the good sense to rework this material into a new context, first into the *New Year Letter*'s idea of a double focus, and then to observe:

> The various "kerygmas," of Blake, of Lawrence, of Freud, of Marx, to which, along with most middle-class intellectuals of my generation, I paid attention between twenty and thirty, had one thing in common. They were all Christian heresies; that is to say, one

[6] *Horizon*, no. 93–94 (October, 1947), as quoted in Richard Hoggart, *Auden, an Introductory Essay* (New Haven: Yale University Press, 1951), p. 136.

cannot imagine their coming into existence except in a civilization which claimed to be based, religiously, on the belief that the Word was made flesh and dwelt among us, and that, in consequence, matter, the natural order, is real and redeemable, not a shadowy appearance or the cause of evil, and historical time is real and significant, not meaningless or an endless series of cycles. . . .

I have come to realize that what is true in what they [the "heretics"] say is implicit in the Christian doctrine of the nature of man, and that what is not Christian is not true; but each of them brought to some particular aspect of life that intensity of attention characteristic of one-sided geniuses (needless to say, they all contradicted each other), and such comprehension of Christian wisdom as I have, little though it be, would be very much less without them.[7]

Even though Auden's conversion represented a major reevaluation of his past, one remains skeptical of Auden's new-found "answer," because it seems to tie up reality and thought, as did Auden's other "answers," into such a neat and final package; Christianity had intellectually "one-upped" Blake, Freud, Lawrence, and Marx by including and harmonizing them all within its intellectual framework. Nor is Auden's statement of his personal experience with this new alternative to frivolity wholly convincing: "And

[7] Untitled essay in *Modern Canterbury Pilgrims*, ed. James Pike (New York: Morehouse-Gorham, 1956), pp. 38–39. For a fuller discussion of the way old material was absorbed into a new context, see Monroe Spears, *The Poetry of W. H. Auden* (New York: Oxford University Press), pp. 171–185.

then, providentially—for the occupational disease of poets is frivolity—I was forced to know in person what it is like to feel oneself the prey of demonic powers, in both the Greek and the Christian sense, stripped of self-control and self-respect, behaving like a ham actor in a Strindberg play."[8] The image of the ham actor and Auden's knowledge of the traditions behind the fear he feels—he began his swerve toward faith by reading theology, in particular Kierkegaard—as well as the difficulty of picturing him as the "prey of demonic powers," create a doubt about Auden's alteration beyond role-play by the influx of the irrational and the divine. But perhaps the conversion of any socially adept, articulate, and sophisticated man would always seem suspicious to the world, and, in any case, the question of Auden's faith may well lie permanently beyond the reach of literary criticism.

Auden's conversion can in one way be fruitfully considered by criticism: although to evaluate the authenticity of the immediate experience is impossible, one can ask if it contributed to the development not just of new ideas, but also of a more judicious way of using these ideas, a new and more fully realized poetic voice. That Auden's major poetry—both his most ambitious longer poems and his most satisfying shorter ones—came after his conversion indicates this; more important still is that, after Auden's initial and often unsteady experimentation with religious poetry, he developed a verse of baroque playfulness and comic meditation that has remained to the present day his major poetic voice.

[8] Pike, p. 41.

One of the most effective ways of tracing Auden's development as a poet is to consider how successfully his poetic language, which always involves some implicit or explicit deprecation of itself as such, manages to refer to forms of truth that exist outside language. The Mortmere mode, with its privacy and aggressive parodic undercutting of both reality and itself, did not strive to achieve any firm outside reference. Poems like "Out on the lawn I lie in bed" attempted to check the Mortmerian fantasy and ground themselves in a utopian drama, which had for its basis the systems of Freud and Marx; the greatest danger in this attempt lay in the fact that, despite Auden's effort to achieve a nonpropagandistic, parabolic art, he involved himself too often in a logical and tonal inconsistency, in that he tried, after exposing the deceptiveness of poetic language, to assert instead a quasi-poetic utopian myth as truth. *Letters from Iceland* managed to solve the dilemma temporarily, by creating for itself a mythic, holiday world that was neither devoid of social reference nor forced to negate itself through parody; "Spain 1937," however, was a reversion to former problems because poetic language and political reality were finally antagonistic. Similarly unsatisfactory are a number of Auden's early attempts at an explicitly religious literature; for example, "Returning each morning from a timeless world" and even "The Meditation of Simeon" are tonally uneasy; there remains an antagonism between playfulness of rhetoric and idea and religious motivation, between virtuosity and spiritual earnestness. The poem of the "middle period" most totally successful and revealing of the poetic voice of the later poetry is the narrator's closing speech in *For the Time Being:* it represents the development of what can be called an explicitly secular voice, one that takes the human, conditional world for its theme and remains comically humble in the knowledge of its own provisionality. Two aspects of this voice can be isolated: first, it creates a tone that resolves in itself both public reference and private community, and, second, it achieves a new and more satisfyingly indirect fusion of the poetic language with extrapoetic truth, of fiction with a reality beyond fiction.

Most striking about the narrator's voice is the sense of a public privacy—the assertion, in the public world, of the intimacy of a small group. Auden has found a voice that can inclusively and intimately make use of the pronoun "we"; in sketching in the typical detail of the conditional world which reemerges just after the celebration of Christmas, he indicates a world of profoundly and comically shared experience. In the uncomfortably prosaic, one finds, if it exists anywhere in contemporary Western society, the point for the communion of mankind; the attempt of Auden's later verse to bring poetry as close as possible to the language of prose is an attempt with implications for not only the form but also the tone and content of his poetry. In this shared world, Auden's virtuosic talent for seeing life in terms of all that is already stylized assumes a positive function: in the stereotype wittily rendered Auden finds one of the surest points for social cohesion in a world where philosophic and spiritual unity is lacking. Thus, the narrator's witty rendering of all the irritations and failures of the temporal world does not become, as does much of the earlier poetry, a display of exhibitionist wit; exhibitionism is tempered to a deeper comic affection for all the familiar imperfections of the world.

What lies behind the achievement of this voice of public privacy is not difficult to determine; Auden has discovered for himself a complex and yet not internally antagonistic poetic identity. He adopts the persona of the discomfited bourgeois, suffering from the 8:15 and living in a world without metaphysic or effective religion; at the same time, he brings to bear on this world a civilized, somewhat aristocratic wit, that of a highly cultured man living in an age of humorous barbarism. The two indentities are then united in a marvelously rich way: the assumption of a bourgeois identity is an act of affectionate humility for the man of wit and learning, which then allows that educated wit the pleasure of turning vulgar reality into baroque and comic form. Even when Auden attacks his new social enemy, the managers, it is from this complex standpoint; the managers are the figures whom all members of a bureaucratic society suspect and dislike, but Auden attacks them by means of a wit that juxtaposes them to their far more impressive and awesome forerunners, the rulers of an aristocratic era. This attack has none of the stridency of a rebel rejecting his society; both the revolutionary hostility to the bourgeois world and the revolutionary dream of a classless society have been abandoned in favor of a complex expression of comic, personal, yet generally shared dislike. What emerges is a paradoxically Arcadian attitude: the detail of the managers' world is sketched in with an irony that so enjoys itself and the communal attitudes it expresses, that one feels the very flaws and commonness of this world to be part of an ideal order. This partly mythic, partly real realm is precarious, being only one step from international disaster; at the same time, as long as it remains within moderate bounds, it indicates, as do limestone landscapes, a faultless world.

That Auden is able to remain so comfortably and lovingly within this realm of flawed flawlessness and mythic realism depends on his new definition of the sphere of poetic language and its relationship to extrapoetic truth. What is implicit in the tone of later poems is explicit in the narrator's closing speech in *For the Time Being;* both the human world and the world of poetic language exist in an affectionately, frivolously, and profoundly ironic relationship to divine reality. The ironic relationship is not a divisive one; on the contrary, it is one in which "God will cheat no one, not even the world of its triumph."[9] The poet works with a medium that is hopelessly corrupt; not only has language been debased in a world of "mass education and mass media,"[10] but is also in essence a medium of artifice and fiction. As such, language cannot refer in any direct manner to truth; to bear witness to truth, poetry must be, as Auden argues in his T. S. Eliot lectures of 1967, "indirect and negative."[11] More explicitly, "sanctity, it would seem, can only be hinted at by comic indirection, as in *Don Quixote.*"[12] In this way, the resources of language can be utilized and simultaneously qualified without a necessity

[9] *The Collected Poetry* p. 466.
[10] Auden, *Secondary Worlds* (New York: Random House, 1968), p. 127. Reprinted by permission of Faber and Faber, Ltd., and Random House, Inc.; copyright ©, 1968, by W. H. Auden.
[11] Ibid., p. 136.
[12] Ibid., p. 139.

for the disturbing self-retraction of much of Auden's work; its conditional nature, underscored by a comedy of sheer linguistic play, hints at a realm beyond the merely conditional. Thus the self-deprecating imagination can exercise itself to its fullest without disturbing what is ultimately real and ultimately nonpoetic.

This theory of the relationship of secular language to divine truth has not taken Auden beyond poetic pose and experimentation with ideas into some final kind of belief; he has found in it, however, the most successful solution to a persistent problem in his poetry. Whatever that outside truth may be, it holds generally true that a subtlety of reference to it makes the poem of particular aesthetic interest; as much as possible, Auden's notorious schoolmasterly voice disappears in favor of a process of indirection that becomes almost satisfying in and of itself. In poems like the narrator's last speech in *For the Time Being* Auden most nearly achieves his goal: the sacred is preserved almost intact outside the poetry, and, within, one finds realized a verbal and intellectual pleasure so pure that one feels as if the lowly human faculty of mere enjoyment had been somehow ennobled. Because of the lowliness of this chief source of pleasure in Auden's work, he will always be criticized; for the same reason he will always be admired.

Index

W. H. Auden as a Social Poet

Designed by R. E. Rosenbaum.
Composed by York Composition Co., Inc.
in 11 point linotype Janson, 3 points leaded,
with display lines in Centaur.
Printed letterpress from type by York Composition Co.
on P & S Offset text, 60 pound basis.
Bound by Vail-Ballou Press
in Holliston book cloth
and stamped in All Purpose foil.

Library of Congress Cataloging in Publication Data

Buell, Frederick, date.
    W. H. Auden as a social poet.
    Includes bibliographical references.
    1. Auden, Wystan Hugh, 1907–   —Political and social views. I.
    Title.
PR6001.U4Z628   821'.9'12   72-12283
ISBN 0-8014-0762-1